Blood,
Bullets,
and
Bones

Blood, Bullets, and Bones

the STORY of
FORENSIC SCIENCE
from SHERLOCK HOLMES *to* DNA

BRIDGET HEOS

BALZER + BRAY
An Imprint of HarperCollinsPublishers

Balzer + Bray is an imprint of HarperCollins Publishers.

Library of Congress Cataloging-in-Publication Data

Names: Heos, Bridget, author.

Title: Blood, bullets, and bones : the story of forensic science from Sherlock Holmes to
 DNA / Bridget Heos.

Description: First edition. | New York : Balzer + Bray, 2016.

Identifiers: LCCN 2016013282 | ISBN 9780062387622 (hardback)

Subjects: LCSH: Forensic sciences—History—Juvenile literature. | BISAC: JUVENILE
 NONFICTION / Science & Nature / General (see also headings under Animals or
 Technology). | JUVENILE NONFICTION / Technology / General. | JUVENILE
 NONFICTION / Law & Crime.

Classification: LCC HV8073.8 .H46 2016 | DDC 363.25—dc23 LC record available at
 https://lccn.loc.gov/2016013282

Typography by Jenna Stempel

21 22 PC/LSCH 10 9 8 7 6 5

❖

First Edition

To my partner in crime, Justin

Contents

Introduction:
From Darkness to Light

At 3:45 a.m. on August 31, 1888, Mary Ann "Polly" Nichols was found dead in a London gateway—one of the first victims of Jack the Ripper. Just half an hour before, a policeman had walked by the gateway and found it empty. The murder must have occurred minutes before the body was discovered. So where was the killer now?

At first, police investigated those connected to Nichols—her ex-husband, for instance. But he had no motive. By now, he and Polly were living separate lives: he was caring for four of their five children near Old Kent Road in South London, and she was living as a prostitute in the East End. When three more victims were found the next month—all prostitutes and all with similar wounds—police knew the killer must be a stranger. Even today, stranger killings are difficult to solve. That was true more so then, when forensic science was in its infancy. The case poses the question: If the London detectives had had the tools that modern forensic scientists have, would Jack the Ripper be known today by his real name? Would some of his victims' lives have been saved?

An 1888 issue of the *Penny Illustrated Paper* features sketches of one of Jack the Ripper's victims and the suspected killer.

Perhaps. But the fact is, today's forensic science is built on innovations of the past. At the time of the Jack the Ripper murders, detectives did use several cutting-edge techniques, including crime scene photography and criminal profiling. Later, investigators would add to these, creating an arsenal of scientific tools that would help catch dangerous criminals. Techniques now include gathering trace evidence; testing bodies for poison; conducting autopsies; studying decomposed bodies; examining blood evidence; profiling criminals; testing DNA evidence; and analyzing bones, fingerprints, and markings on bullets.

Put simply, forensic science is the use of science to solve crimes. Though the following mysteries may seem to be ripped from the pages of crime novels, they are very real. Each describes the tragic taking—and breaking—of lives. That's why forensic science is so important: it brings about justice for victims, peace of mind for communities, just punishment for the guilty, and freedom for the innocent.

Forensic science is far from perfect, however. As DNA testing became available, it helped to prove hundreds of prisoners innocent when, in many cases, less accurate forensic science methods such as bite mark analysis had been used to convict them in the first place. Forensic science disciplines are now being reviewed to determine their validity and to ensure that experts are clear about what forensic science can and can't tell us.

Soon after the dawn of DNA evidence, forensic science invaded pop culture. It was propelled by the popularity of *CSI: Crime Scene Investigation*, which first aired in 2000 and unleashed a wave of similar crime shows. But forensic science is actually older than most people might think. In fact, it's ancient. *A Book of Criminal Cases*, written around 270 CE, describes the work of Zhang Ju, a Chinese coroner who solved murders through the careful examination of victims' bodies. In one case, he needed to determine whether a man had died in a fire or was murdered and then placed in the fire to cover up the crime. The coroner put two pigs in a fire, one alive and the other dead. Then he examined the pigs' bodies. The pig that died in the fire had ashes in its mouth; the pig that was already dead didn't. The man didn't have ashes in his mouth either, proving to Zhang Ju that the victim must have been dead prior to the fire. Later in China, the book *The Washing Away of Wrongs* provided a textbook to other coroners. For instance, it described how to tell if a person had died from drowning or had been dumped in the water postmortem.

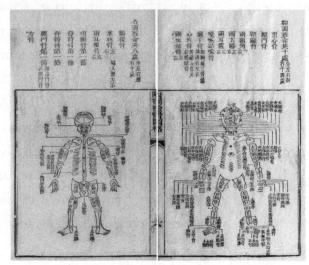

Anatomical diagrams from *The Washing Away of Wrongs,*
a thirteenth-century Chinese crime-solving manual

Unfortunately, such ingenious forensic science didn't spread throughout the world. In England during the Middle Ages, crimes were examined by a crowner, so named because he was appointed by the crown, or king, and seized the property of criminals for the crown. In the case of murder, the crowner (which term gradually changed to the modern word coroner) was also charged with examining the body and investigating the crime—but to little avail, as he was neither a doctor nor a detective, but essentially a money collector. Crime wasn't investigated in any scientific way. The focus instead was on punishment. Whoever the crowner pointed a finger at was arrested and tortured or killed. Well into the 1800s, people were hanged publicly for murder, but also for minor offenses like pickpocketing. This was thought to deter crime, but even at the hangings, pickpocketing was rampant. It was clear that a new system was needed—both to eliminate cruel and unusual punishment and to ensure that when grave crimes did occur, the right people were punished. Crime needed to be fought not with fear but with science.

The Idle Prentice Executed at Tyburn, plate 11 from *Industry and Idleness* by William Hogarth, depicts the rampant pickpocketing that occurred at hangings in the 1700s.

1

A Whiff of Garlic:
The First Poison Tests

Some of the first scientific tests related to murder cases were for poison, and arsenic in particular. Arsenic has been called "inheritance powder" and "widow-maker" for its popularity among murderers of the greedy variety. It was a favorite weapon because it made the death look like it was from natural causes. Before modern plumbing and safe food handling, serious stomach ailments like dysentery and typhoid fever were common, and even healthy people could suddenly die from these diseases. So if someone suffered from a bout of vomiting and diarrhea, it would likely be chalked up to illness. Even when suspicions arose, there were no tests for poison. All that changed with Mary Blandy, an Englishwoman accused of poisoning her own father in 1751.

Mary's father, Francis Blandy, was seeking a nobleman for her to marry. To attract the best of suitors, Mr. Blandy started a rumor that his daughter's dowry was £10,000 (more than $1 million today), though, in fact, he had little money. Mary had several men interested, all of whom her father deemed subpar. Finally, she met Captain William Henry Cranstoun and fell in love. Her father swooned, too—William was the son of a lord and lady. Little did father or daughter know that the fine young gentleman would be their undoing.

In 1747, a year after the couple met, William proposed to Mary but also shared some troubling news. A Scottish woman was claiming to be his wife. Mary believed William when he assured her that it wasn't true, but she didn't tell her father. Mr. Blandy found out in a letter from William's great-uncle. At first, Mary's father believed William's story, too, or went along with it anyway, apparently swayed by the young man's good name. Mr. Blandy was supposedly overheard saying that he hoped to one day be the grandfather of a lord. And so the engagement continued—for a while. But when a year passed and William still hadn't straightened out his marital problems, Mr. Blandy grew impatient. He ordered Mary to break things off until William was free to marry. (In fact, he never would be. Unbeknownst to the Blandys, the courts had said that William was to remain married to his wife in Scotland.)

With Mr. Blandy standing firm, things took a murderous turn. William sent Mary a packet of chemicals that he called a "love philter," which would supposedly change her father's mind about their engagement. First, Mary put the potion in her father's tea, but when he left it untouched, two of the maids, Susan Gunnell and Ann Emmet, drank the remains and became violently ill. Mary then put the potion in her father's gruel. He ate the gruel twice in one day, vomiting violently both times. Because Mary nonetheless insisted that a new pot of gruel not be made, Susan became suspicious and told Mr. Blandy that Mary must be trying to poison him. Mr. Blandy urged his daughter to confess, to no avail.

Still, the evidence was mounting. Some of the servants found a packet of chemicals that had belonged to Mary in the embers of the fireplace. By now, Dr. Anthony Addington had been called in to care for the patient. Addington agreed with the servants that Mr. Blandy was suffering from poison. The doctor was determined to prove it, too, through a simple sniff test. When heated, arsenic gives off a garlic odor. Addington threw the packet of chemicals onto a hot iron, and indeed, it emitted a whiff of garlic. Though the test would not be considered definitive today, it was groundbreaking at the time.

Meanwhile, feeling the case closing in on her, Mary wrote a letter of warning to William:

Dear Willy:

My father is so bad, that I have only time to tell you, that if you do not hear from me soon again, don't be frightened. I am better myself. Lest any accident should happen to your letters, take care what you write. My sincere compliments. I am ever yours.[1]

This letter was discovered before it could be sent and was shown to Mr. Blandy, who rather forgivingly said, "Poor love-sick girl! What will not a woman do for the man she loves?"[2]

Finally feeling a change of heart, Mary apologized to her father for making him deathly ill, but she denied knowing what the powder would do. Mr. Blandy forgave her and died three days later. The courts would not be so understanding. Addington testified that the powder was arsenic, and Mary was found guilty. When she was brought to the hangman on April 6, 1752, she asked him not to hang her too high, lest the onlookers see up her skirt. Mary may have been a murderer, but she was a modest murderer.

MISS BLANDY *at the place of Execution near Oxford, attended by the Revd Mr Swinton*

The execution of Miss Mary Blandy

Through the years, tests for arsenic became more exact. In 1806, Dr. Valentine Rose, a professor of medicine in Berlin, developed a test that didn't require samples of the poisonous substance. Instead, the corpse could be tested. First, the stomach was cut up and boiled until it was liquid. The liquid was then filtered and treated with nitric acid. This converted arsenic into arsenious oxide, for which there was a known test. Rose's test led to the conviction of one of Germany's most prolific serial killers, Anna Zwanziger.

Orphaned at age five, Anna moved from family member to family member in her native Bavaria (now a part of Germany). At age fifteen she married a much older lawyer, who was an alcoholic. When he could no longer support Anna and their two children, she became a high-end call girl. Her husband died, and Anna's prostitution led to a pregnancy and adoption. After that ordeal, Anna gave up prostitution and went to work as a maid, with the intention of marrying one of her employers.

Her first position was with Justice Wolfgang Glaser, who had recently separated from his wife. The wife soon returned, however, and a jealous Anna began poisoning her. Mrs. Glaser died a month later, but it wasn't the happy ending Anna had hoped for. Wolfgang never proposed. Anna moved on to the home of Justice Grohmann. He was ill when she arrived and died of a violent stomach ailment soon after. Her next job was for Justice Gebhard and his pregnant wife. Soon after giving birth, she, too, became sick. On her deathbed she accused Anna of poisoning her, but apparently that wasn't enough to rouse the judge's suspicions. When friends of the judge fell ill while visiting the house, they blamed Anna as well. The judge finally sent her packing.

Before leaving, Anna prepared coffee for two of the maids and milk for the baby. Oddly, no one questioned the safety of drinks prepared by an accused poisoner, and all three ingested them and became very sick. Thankfully, they recovered, and Anna's treacherous farewell became her undoing. Police were called in and found arsenic in the salt box, which they believed to be the source of the poison in the drinks. They tracked down Anna, who had two packets of poison with her. Mrs. Glaser's body was exhumed, and investigators used Rose's test to find arsenic in her stomach. Anna confessed and was beheaded in 1811.

In spite of better and more frequent tests for poison, its use as a murder weapon remained common throughout the nineteenth century. To stop would-be poisoners, England enacted the Arsenic Act in 1851. Under the new laws, druggists could sell arsenic only by prescription, or to customers they knew personally. Arsenic sales had to be recorded in a poison register, and arsenic was to be colored with soot or blue indigo so that it wouldn't be mistaken for flour or sugar.

The new laws didn't stop Mary Ann Cotton, who was either one of Britain's most prolific serial killers or the world's unluckiest woman. In all, three husbands, ten children, five stepchildren, her mother, her sister-in-law, and a lover died of illnesses, most while in Cotton's care. Some of the deaths may have been natural, but others were certainly not. Her final spree occurred in 1871, when within a short span, her husband, child, stepson, and lover all died of stomach ailments. Mary Ann was left with one stepson, Charles. Hoping to marry again, she consulted with a government official, Thomas Riley, about putting Charles in a workhouse (homes for the poor that had horrible working and living conditions). Riley said it could be arranged, but only if Mary Ann went with the boy. Mary Ann balked at the idea and said, "I won't be troubled long. He'll go like all the rest of the Cotton family."[3] That shocked Riley, as the boy looked perfectly healthy. Less than a week later, Charles died with Mary Ann by his bedside; she was supposedly trying to nurse him back to health.

Riley reported his conversation with Mary Ann to the police, who ordered a coroner's inquiry and an autopsy. But it was rather a rush job. Dr. Kilburn, and his assistant, Dr. Chalmers, examined the body just an hour before the inquest began—on a table in Mary Ann's house, no less. At first, they ruled the death to be from natural causes, and the boy was buried. But that was not the end of that. Dr. Kilburn had brought home the boy's stomach and stored it in a cupboard. Around that time, newspapers began reporting that Mary

Ann was a poisoner. Dr. Kilburn decided that perhaps he should test that stomach after all. It was riddled with arsenic. Mary Ann was arrested.

The other bodies from the Cotton house were exhumed and found to contain arsenic as well, but Mary Ann went on trial only for the murder of Charles, whose case was the strongest. It was learned that she had gotten around signing the poison registry by sending a child to buy the arsenic, and when that didn't work, a neighbor. Her defense attorneys claimed that fumes from the wall-paper (which at the time commonly contained arsenic) had caused the deaths. The jury didn't buy it. After deliberating for only an hour, they found Mary Ann guilty of murder, and on March 24, 1873, she was hanged.

People sometimes cope with evil and tragedy in strange ways. When Mary Ann was hanged, children made up a song about her:

> Mary Ann Cotton
> She's dead and she's rotten.
> She lies in her bed
> With her eyes wide oppen;
> Sing, sing, oh what can I sing?
> Mary Ann Cotton is tied up with a string.
> Where? Where? Up in the air
> Sellin' black puddings a penny a pair. [4]

(Black pudding is a kind of sausage that is popular in Great Britain.)

Though forensic science eventually stopped Cotton in her

murderous tracks, the fact that Charles may have been her twenty-first victim—and that his murder was found out only after the press ran stories about Mary Ann—shows that the system for detecting foul play wasn't working. That was true in America as well as Europe. Case in point: the 1895 death of Evelina Bliss—allegedly at the hands of her own daughter—was investigated solely because of a chance visit from a friend.

Life hadn't gone as planned for Mary Alice Livingston. She had grown up wealthy and well educated and had a vivacious personality. Yet in an age when marrying well was the key to establishing oneself socially and financially, her first relationship had resulted in a pregnancy—but no marriage. That happened a second time . . . and a third. Ten years later, she found herself pregnant with her fourth. Though unmarried, she went by Mary Alice Fleming to avoid the stigma of never having wed.

To top things off, her own mother was on her case. A fourth pregnancy with no husband? How would she afford that? She couldn't support the children she already had. Mary Alice was living in a hotel in Harlem—supported by her stepfather, Henry Bliss (who was separated from Mrs. Bliss). Mary Alice's father had been Robert Swift Livingston, a wealthy landowner who had married Mrs. Bliss when she was a teenager and he was eighty-one. When he died, he left Mary Alice and her mother money, but Mary Alice wouldn't have access to her $80,000 share (more than $2 million today) until the death of Mrs. Bliss. The mother and daughter lived close to each other, and on Friday, August 30, 1895, Mary Alice sent Mrs. Bliss some clam chowder. Whether it was an act of kindness or murder is at the crux of this case.

That day, Mary Alice's ten-year-old daughter, Gracie, had gone to her friend Florence's house, her fourteen-month-old sibling in tow. Walter, Mary Alice's teenage son, was hanging out with friends downtown. Mary Alice ordered room service from the Colonial Hotel Restaurant—clam chowder and lemon meringue pie. When the girls returned to the hotel room with the toddler, Mary Alice sent them with the pie and a tin pail of chowder to Mrs. Bliss's house. The grandmother welcomed the girls inside, poured the soup into a pitcher, and sent the pail home with the girls.

When they returned to the hotel, Mary Alice said, "I hope you didn't eat any of it."

"No, Ma," Gracie said. [5]

Then Mary Alice served dinner—more room service. Afterward, the girls took the baby to play in the park. They returned after dark, and Florence walked home.

Meanwhile, Mrs. Bliss had fallen violently ill. A family friend, Augustus Teubner, happened to drop by her apartment and immediately called for a doctor.

When Dr. William Bullman arrived, Mrs. Bliss told him, "I am going to die. I have been poisoned by my relatives, who are trying to get my money." [6]

She said the poison had been in the clam chowder. Her condition worsened, and at eleven p.m., she died. Bullman examined the pitcher that had contained the chowder and found white residue at the bottom. He saved the pitcher and some of the vomit for analysis and informed police of a possible poisoning. Had it not been for the friend's visit, Mrs. Bliss would have died alone, and since autopsies weren't routine, it probably would have been ruled a natural death.

Instead, poison was found in the body, as well as in the pitcher. Mary Alice stood her ground, insisting, "I am entirely innocent. My mother was the best friend I had."[7]

Detectives didn't buy it. They arrested Mary Alice after her mother's funeral. Mary Alice quickly became front-page news. Reporters learned that although she went by Mary Alice Fleming, she'd never been married to a Fleming or anyone else. Instead, two men had promised marriage but backed out. Newspapers blamed Mary Alice for this, calling her a degenerate.

But by the time the trial began, the press had done an about-face. By now, Mary Alice had had her baby. Instead of painting her as the murderous daughter, the press began referring to her as a single mother whose children would be orphaned if she were sent to the electric chair. They described her every blush, smile, and whisper in court, as though she were the heroine in a romance novel. They even published the love letters she'd written to the father of her two youngest children, which were read in court. The prosecution hoped they would show that Mary Alice hated her mother—and they certainly did show anger toward her and her lover's families for interfering in their romance, but they also showed a woman in love. The newspapers breathlessly reported all of this.

The prosecution put forth the theory that Mary Alice had poisoned the clam chowder and then sent it to her mother via her daughter. Their expert witness was Dr. Walter Scheele, a chemist who had tested Mrs. Bliss's stomach, the sediment in the pitcher, and a tea tray and Japanese jar found with Mary Alice's belongings in the apartment building (which she denied owning). He said that all of these contained arsenic. The state also called experts to say that Mrs.

Bliss's symptoms were characteristic of arsenic poisoning.

With the money Mary Alice had inherited after her mother's death, she hired a crack defense attorney, Charles Brooke. He attacked Scheele on every front, calling character witnesses who said they wouldn't believe a word Scheele said, and another witness who claimed Scheele said he would fix the evidence to prove Mary Alice guilty. Brooke further argued that if Mary Alice had poisoned the chowder, she wouldn't have sent it with her daughter for fear that the daughter might eat it.

He offered an alternative theory for why Mrs. Bliss had arsenic in her system: she was an arsenic eater. This was known as the Styrian defense. Strange as it may seem, people in the Styrian Alps along the border of Austria and Hungary purposely ate arsenic. Though the practice was illegal, bootleggers sold arsenic oxide as a paste that people would spread on their bread like butter. Beginning in childhood, the Styrians built up a tolerance by taking half a grain (30 milligrams) two to three times a week and increasing the dosage until they reached five grains (300 milligrams) or even more—enough to kill most people. It wasn't to defend themselves against the possibility of one day being poisoned (à la the Dread Pirate Roberts in *The Princess Bride*). Rather, they believed arsenic enhanced health and beauty. In women, it caused a pleasant plumpness, and in men, vitality. It also caused goiters and birth defects (as arsenic interferes with iodine in the body) and probably cancer. In other words, eating poison wasn't actually good for the Styrians.

Nonetheless, the practice of eating arsenic spread to America—sort of. The Styrian arsenic eaters were featured in both the popular press and in medical journals. Arsenic became a popular ingredient in cosmetic products, including face powder, hair powder, and even pills for improving the complexion. Dr. Campbell's Safe Arsenic Complexion Wafers were sold over the counter under several different names. Though they contained little arsenic, there were newspaper reports of women dying after taking too many. Besides being a really bad idea for those who took them, these "safe" arsenic pills also provided a defense for those accused of murder: that the victim habitually ate arsenic for good health or the Styrian defense.

Advertisement for Dr. Campbell's
Safe Arsenic Complexion Wafers

After twelve hours of deliberating, the jury found Mary Alice not guilty. Whether they questioned the honesty of the expert witness, accepted the Styrian defense, liked Mary Alice too much to believe that she could murder her own mother, or simply did not want to see a mother of four put to death is unknown.

Juries at the time were indeed skeptical of scientific testimony. And it wasn't just them. The courts were wary of it, too. In another prominent murder-by-poison case, a jury convicted the accused, but a state supreme court overturned the verdict, believing the forensic evidence to be weak. Thomas Swope (nicknamed Colonel Swope) had earned his fortune in real estate and owned more land than anyone in Kansas City, Missouri. A bachelor, he was close to his nieces and nephews, and several lived with him in his mansion in nearby Independence. They were set to inherit at least part of his $3.5-million estate (about $94 million today) upon their uncle's death.

In the fall of 1909, Swope suffered a minor injury, and Dr. Bennett Clark Hyde came to the mansion to care for him. Hyde was married to Swope's niece Frances, but he hadn't exactly been accepted into the family

Exterior shot of Swope mansion in Independence, Missouri

with open arms. Though he was the president of the Jackson County Medical Society, Hyde also had a scandalous history of grave robbing and horribly mistreating a patient. As part of his treatment of Colonel Swope, Hyde prescribed a digestive capsule. Twenty minutes later, Swope suffered from convulsions. A nurse reported that he said, "Oh, my God, I wish I were dead. I wish I had not taken that medicine."[8] Several hours later, he died.

Soon after, several members of the Swope household came down with typhoid fever, and Hyde again stayed at the house to play doctor. In early December, Colonel Swope's nephew Chrisman Swope suffered from the same type of convulsions as his uncle and died. Hyde insisted on staying on to care for other family members, but his success rate left much to be desired. Several of the nurses gave Frances's mother, Mrs. Logan Swope, an ultimatum: If Hyde continued to care for the family, they would leave. One nurse, Miss Houlehan, put it plainly: "People are being murdered in this house." [9]

Indeed, the family did ask Hyde to leave on December 18. They also had the bodies of Colonel and Chrisman exhumed and sent

Dr. Bennett Clark Hyde, the Swope family doctor and husband of Frances Swope

to Chicago for autopsies. Meanwhile, Hyde's wife, Frances, hired a team of defense attorneys (which happens to have included my great-uncle R. R. Brewster, who passed away decades before I was born). The trial began April 16, 1910. Prosecutors theorized that Swope had planned to change his will so that his money went to charity, rather than to his nieces and nephews. When Hyde learned of this, he killed Swope to secure Frances's share of the money.

The state called many expert witnesses, who concurred that the evidence pointed to poisonings. For instance, the pathologists from Chicago, Dr. Walter Haines and Dr. Victor Vaughan, testified that they found strychnine in the liver, and a trace of cyanide. Other evidence was equally damning. Hyde had purchased cyanide capsules and digestive capsules. He explained that the cyanide was purchased to kill cockroaches, to which the prosecutor replied, "Does a man kill cockroaches with poison capsules?"[10]

Prosecutors argued that, more likely, Hyde had opened both capsules and exchanged the cyanide in one with the digestive medicine in the other. Hyde had also purchased typhoid fever capsules, which he said were for experiments, but the fact that several family members contracted typhoid fever was suspicious, to say the least. On May 16, the jury found Hyde guilty.

His lawyers appealed the case to the Supreme Court of Missouri, where the case was remanded. Hyde would get a new trial. The appeal was granted largely because of what the justices saw as weak expert testimony. They said that a lethal dose of strychnine should have killed a healthy man within a couple of hours, and cyanide in less time, but that Colonel Swope, who was in his eighties and in poor health, had survived for ten hours after taking the pill. The justices objected to the state's theory that when mixed, the two poisons counteracted each other. After all, the prosecution's own experts knew of no cases in which this had happened, and it was counterintuitive. Furthermore, the justices said that whereas Hyde was shown to have purchased cyanide, only a trace of that poison was found in Colonel Swope. There was no evidence showing that Hyde had purchased strychnine, the poison that was found in a greater quantity. (In Chrisman, only a trace of strychnine and no cyanide were found.)

As for the autopsies, the judges objected to the fact that the pathologist didn't have a witness with him during parts of the autopsy and that the defendant was never allowed to have his own experts examine the organs. The justices could have overturned the verdict without allowing a second trial, but they gave the prosecutors a second chance. As it turned out, they would need more than that.

The second trial ended in a mistrial. The jurors were sequestered in a hotel when one juror went AWOL, hopping a train and wandering the countryside for two days before going home to his wife. She brought him back to the courthouse, where he explained that he had needed some fresh air—and freedom from the staring eyes of the courthouse. He claimed not to have discussed the trial while away, but the judge couldn't be sure of that. He *was* pretty sure that the juror was suffering from a mental illness. Considering all this, the judge declared a mistrial.

The third trial resulted in a hung jury. Before the fourth trial, Hyde's attorneys pointed out that a person can't be tried more than three times for the same criminal charge. Hyde went free. Frances Swope stood by Hyde throughout the court ordeal, prompting him to say, "I have learned that a man can stand anything with a wife like mine believing in him and sustaining him."[11] Not to mention paying for his attorneys.

By the early twentieth century, reliable poison tests were available. But these cases show that forensic evidence wasn't enough to get a conviction—it had to be strong enough to withstand the scrutiny of judge and jury. The dots had to be connected from the manner of death to the poison found in the victim's body to the poison being acquired by the suspect. Even then, unscientific factors came into play: a persuasive attorney, a questioned reputation, a likeable suspect, the gut feelings of a jury, a well-crafted appeal. That's still true today.

What has changed is that all unexplained deaths are now

investigated by medical examiners, so that foul play isn't detected only when somebody gets suspicious—or, in the case of Evelina Bliss, by the chance visit of a friend. Once established, the medical examiner's office also hired the best toxicologists, so that expert testimony became more accurate and not as easily questioned by the defense. The rise of the medical examiner—and the fall of those who would have gotten away with murder—is the subject of the next chapter.

L'AFFAIRE DES POISONS

Having no test for poison didn't just allow murderers to go free. It also led to false convictions. Nowhere was that more true than during the French scandal known as *L'Affaire des Poisons* (the Affair of the Poisons). It began in 1672, when Marie Madeleine D'Aubray, Marquise de Brinvilliers, was accused of poisoning her father and two brothers to gain inheritance money.

A married woman, she'd been having an affair with a man named Gaudin de Sainte-Croix. To discourage the affair, her father had Gaudin sentenced to the Bastille for six weeks. There, the unscrupulous Gaudin met an Italian poisoner known only as Exili. Upon his release from prison, Gaudin set up his own poison lab and supplied Marie with poison to kill her father in 1666 and her brothers in 1670. Then one day, Gaudin dropped dead in his lab, possibly after experimenting on himself. Police discovered letters in the lab from Marie offering to pay for the poison she'd used to kill her family members. She initially fled the country, but later confessed to the murders. In her defense, she argued, "Out of so many guilty people must I be the only one to be put to death? . . . Half the people in town are involved in this sort of thing, and I could ruin them if I were to talk."[12]

The "but everybody else is poisoning their families" argument didn't gain Marie any sympathy—she was beheaded in 1676—but it was an alarming allegation, and French officials took notice. Soon after Marie's death, King Louis XIV appointed the lieutenant general of the Paris Police, Nicolas de la Reynie, to investigate possible poisoners operating in Paris. In alchemist labs across the city, Reynie found poisons such as arsenic, nitric acid, and mercury, and things that were equally incriminating because of their role in black magic and the possibility that they had been acquired by violent means: nail clippings, drops of human blood, and what was supposedly the fat of a hanged man, to name a few.

Nineteenth-century engraving of the beheading
of Marie Madeleine D'Aubray

Suspects were arrested and tortured until they talked. To stop the torture, prisoners would confess to crimes they hadn't committed and accuse those who were innocent. In all, 442 people were charged and 319 ordered arrested. Of course, none of the accusations could be verified scientifically. At the time, the only so-called "poison test" was to feed an animal the last meal of a victim and see if it died. Any such food evidence was long gone. But trials were held nonetheless, in a secret courtroom called the burning chamber (so named because the windows were blackened to avoid prying eyes, and the room was lit by flaming torches). Here, thirty-six people were sentenced to death and many more banished or imprisoned.

Then it all came to a screeching halt. Catherine Deshayes, known as La Voisin (the neighbor), was an accused poisoner with clients in high places. She refused to share information about them, but when police arrested her lover, Le Sage, they convinced him to talk. Le Sage claimed that Louis XIV's beloved mistress, Madame de Montespan, was a client of La Voisin's. La Voisin's daughter (who had also been arrested) accused Montespan of purchasing love potions and offering human sacrifices so that the king would love her more.

Montespan had reason to be jealous. Though she had had seven children with the king and had been his favorite mistress for years (many referred to her as "the real queen of France"), she wasn't the only woman in his life. In addition to his wife, Queen Maria-Thérèse, Louis XIV had a string of mistresses. In fact, he had recently fallen in love with both his children's nanny, Madame de Maintenon, and a noblewoman named Marie Angélique de Scorailles. Marie Angélique became pregnant by him, but sadly lost the child, became ill, and died soon after.

La Voisin's daughter offered a treacherous explanation. She said that when the love potions hadn't worked, Montespan had poisoned Marie Angélique—and had tried to poison the king, too. But it appeared to be another case of the accused saying anything to avoid being tortured. An autopsy was performed, and while poison tests on organs were unavailable at the time, evidence pointed to lung infection—

Portrait of Madame de Montespan (1640–1707)

not poison—having killed Marie Angélique. At any rate, Louis XIV didn't believe the accusations, and wasn't about to have his mistress—favorite or not—raked over the coals. Rather than allow the matter to be made public, he dissolved the burning court. After all, it's one thing to hear unfounded accusations about hundreds of people, but another entirely to hear them against a loved one.

2

Bodies of Evidence: Autopsies
and the Rise of Medical Examiners

In the American West, shootings were commonplace. Drunken arguments in saloons and quarrels over property were deadly affairs. But the Wild West wasn't lawless. After a shooting, the body would be handed over to the coroner, who would handle the investigation (as opposed to a detective). The coroner was an elected official who would summon a jury of male citizens for an inquest. He wasn't usually a doctor, though he might choose a doctor to be a jury member. The coroner and jury would view the body, and if a doctor was present, he might examine the body or even conduct an autopsy. The jury would also listen to witness testimony. If there were witnesses, their word was as good as gold. Whoever they saw draw first was guilty, whereas the second to draw was acting in self-defense. If there was a question of guilt, the case went to trial.

NEWSPAPER

NEW YORK, NOVEMBER 3, 1877.

An 1877 newspaper illustration of a poker game
in a Wyoming saloon

The death of Charles Davis in Eli Signor's bar, as described by a Wyoming coroner in the late 1800s, shows how this worked. According to witnesses, Charles entered the bar at ten a.m. and ordered several rounds of drinks. He stepped away from the bar to eat lunch (many saloons offered free lunch with the purchase of a drink—or in Charles's case, several).

When he returned, the owner, Eli Signor, wasn't behind the bar. Charles called for the "Dam son of a bitch"[1] to get him a drink, and when Signor didn't immediately appear, Charles fired his gun at Signor's cat, threw the barroom chairs into a pile, jumped up on the billiard table, dragged his feet across it, and threw billiard balls across the room.

Signor came to see what the commotion was about. Now, a certain amount of rowdiness was allowed in saloons, where strong whiskey was the order of the day. Cowboys driving cattle from Texas to Montana—far away from family and home—tended to be a wild crowd. Gambling was allowed in saloons and often led to gunfights. Barkeepers made money off this heavy-drinking crowd, and while the whiskey (and money) was flowing, they accepted *some* obnoxious-ness. But Charles's behavior had crossed the line, and Signor said so. Undeterred, Charles told Signor to fix him a drink. Signor agreed to, but only after Charles picked up the chairs. Charles wanted that drink immediately. He grabbed Signor by the collar, pulled his gun on him, and said, "Signor, you Poppy Eyed Bastard, I will fix you."[2]

But Charles had it backward. Signor, who was bent over picking up a chair, grabbed Charles's gun with his left hand and pulled his own gun out of his pocket with his right. He shot Charles four times. According to the witnesses, Charles was reaching for a second gun when Signor fired again—shooting the rowdy customer dead and proving that there really is no such thing as a free lunch.

Based on witness testimony, the jury ruled the shooting a jus-tifiable homicide. Today, a thorough autopsy and crime scene investigation would have been conducted to confirm what witnesses said, but even now, the word of several witnesses, all in agreement, holds a lot of sway in court.

On the other hand, if there were no witnesses, a murder often went unsolved. In a typical case from 1889, the coroner and jury rode out to investigate the dead body of a man found in the open coun-try of Wyoming. (In those days, such an excursion was common.) The coroner later described in his report the body of a thirty-five-to-forty-year-old sandy-haired man badly decomposed, his pockets empty. He declared the cause of death undetermined, and the inves-tigation ended. With empty pockets, was the man robbed and killed? Did he die of dehydration? And for that matter, who was this man? All these questions went unanswered. And this wasn't true just in the Wild West. If a dead body washed up in the East River in New

York, it was just as likely that the coroner's jury would throw up their hands and say, "Who knows what happened?"

This was unfair to the victims and their families and frustrating for the communities where crimes went unsolved. As the *Laramie Daily Boomerang* stated after a man was found shot to death on the side of the road, "It has become a regular thing for a man to be found dead, family murdered, and nothing has been done to apprehend and punish the guilty ones."[3]

From coast to coast, America needed thorough murder investigations using forensic science. That change would come about first in England and the rest of Europe, where the "crowner" (coroner) system had been in place since the year 1000. In those days, the British king was entitled to a share of the property of anyone convicted of a crime. A coroner was a high-ranking official appointed to collect the king's due. Of course, the coroner first had to determine who committed the crime. The sheriff would call the coroner, and the coroner would investigate.

By around 1300, the coroner was summoning a jury to help with the inquisition. Together, they would "view" the body, which is quite different from examining the body through an autopsy. After all, the coroner was not a doctor. Nevertheless, the coroner and his jury would determine the cause of death, interview witnesses, and decide who, if anyone, was responsible. Then the sheriff would make an arrest. In time, the king no longer collected the property of criminals, and the coroner's status fell. He became a workaday government official. And he still wasn't a doctor.

Dr. Thomas Wakley sought to change that. Founder of the prominent British medical journal the *Lancet*, he crusaded on its pages

for all coroners to be doctors. Wakley ran for the office of coroner in his county of Middlesex, but England's coroners, wanting to
keep their jobs, opposed him. After several tries, Wakley was elected,
and by the mid-1800s, all of England was electing doctors to be
their coroners. It just made sense. By the late 1800s, coroners were
investigating any death in which the cause was unknown, violent, or
unnatural. A thorough investigation no longer hinged on suspicion
or luck. It was now a matter of routine, in England, at least.

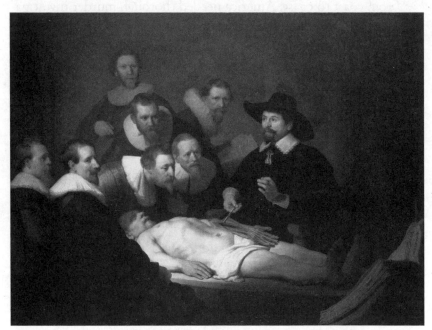

The Anatomy Lesson of Dr. Nicolaes Tulp (1632) by Rembrandt

At the same time, doctors were becoming more knowledgeable
about autopsies. Medical schools across Europe offered courses
in forensic pathology, the study of corpses and causes of death.
Alexandre Lacassagne was a pioneer in this field. He joined the
Institute of Legal Medicine in Lyon, France, in 1881 and began

leading students in dozens of criminal autopsies each year. They learned to read such details on a corpse as whether the victim had been strangled by bare hands or a cord, and from what angle a knife must have been wielded. Besides building a state-of-the-art lab for the student autopsy work, Lacassagne also created a criminal museum at the university. It included fractured skulls, firearms and bullets, a variety of ropes used in hangings, fabrics stained with blood, human and animal hair, and wounded body parts and their corresponding weapons—hatchets, knives, swords, hammers, guns, and more.

At first the public was skeptical as to how forensic pathologists like those trained by Lacassagne could help solve crimes. But in England, the case of Cora Crippen settled any doubts. Hawley Harvey Crippen and his wife, Cora, were Americans living in London. Hawley worked for a mail-order homeopathic medicine company. (Advertised in newspapers and wildly popular, homeopathic medicines were questionably helpful at best and dangerous at worst. Dr. Campbell's Safe Arsenic Complexion Wafers were one such example.) Cora, who went by the stage name Belle Elmore, was an actress and singer. Hawley at first supported Belle's career, but he was fired for being too sidetracked from his own work. He became a dentist, and Belle,

Alexandre Lacassagne, pioneer in the field of forensic pathology

popular for her dramatic flair on and off the stage, was elected treasurer of the Music Hall Ladies' Guild. The couple grew apart. Each struck up an affair, Belle with a boarder the couple had taken in and Hawley with his eighteen-year-old secretary, Ethel Le Neve.

The marriage turned especially sour when Belle heard rumors that Ethel was pregnant. She threatened to expose the affair, ruining Hawley's reputation. But the secret would be safe with Belle, because after a dinner party on January 31, 1910, she was apparently never seen again. Ethel delivered a note to the Ladies' Guild, purportedly from Belle, which said she was resign-

Cora Crippen (stage name Belle Elmore)

ing as treasurer and moving to America to care for a sick relative.

The note seemed fishy to the guild ladies. Belle would have mentioned having a sick relative—the ladies discussed everything together. Their suspicions grew when they saw Ethel wearing Belle's jewelry. The ladies hounded Hawley with questions until he finally told them that Belle had died. This did nothing to quell the guild ladies' inquiries. They asked Hawley when the funeral would be. He said Belle was being cremated. But the ladies knew that a cremation would go against Belle's Catholic sensibility (at the time, the Catholic Church forbade cremation). Continuing their sleuthing, the ladies learned that on the day Belle had supposedly left for America, no such ship had set sail. Furthermore, there was no record of Belle's death in California.

The ladies brought their mounting evidence to Chief Inspector Walter Dew of Scotland Yard. He paid a visit to Crippen on July 8, 1910, and asked him where his wife was. Hawley said that the ladies' suspicions were true: Belle wasn't really dead. Rather, she'd left Hawley for another man. He'd made up the story of her death to avoid embarrassment. Though he'd answered cunningly, the visit had shaken Hawley. Frightened that a police investigation was underway, he fled for Canada the next day with Ethel. When Dew learned that the couple had left town, he conducted a thorough search of the Crippen home.

In the basement, beneath the floor, detectives found a decomposing torso. With evidence pointing to murder, police chased Hawley and Ethel across the Atlantic and arrested them in Canada. Hawley insisted that the torso must have been buried in the basement before he moved into the house. Scotland Yard brought in Bernard Spilsbury to determine whether the body was Belle's. Spilsbury was a prominent pathologist at St. Mary's Hospital, which housed the region's best forensic medicine practice. He found on the torso a scar, which he believed was from a surgery Belle had had. He also found hyoscine, a sedative, in the body tissues.

At the trial, prosecutors put forth the theory that Hawley had called a doctor to say that his wife was ill and then given her hyoscine in the hopes of causing an overdose. Because she'd supposedly already been sick, the death would have looked natural. When the sedative failed to kill Belle, Hawley shot her instead. He then chopped up her body, throwing some parts into the canal, burning others, and burying the torso. Hawley was tried and sentenced to death; Ethel was found innocent of being an accessory. Spilsbury's work proved to the public that autopsies could play an important role in murder cases. But was Spilsbury right?

Ladies' Guild members during the trial of Hawley Harvey Crippen for the murder of his wife, Cora Crippen

Recently, forensic biologist David Foran of Michigan State University decided to investigate the case using DNA evidence. He was skeptical of the prosecutor's theory because in most cases, poisoners follow through with their plan to make the murder look like a natural death. He examined one of the scar tissue slides that Spilsbury described as belonging to Cora. Then Foran took DNA samples from Cora Crippen's living relatives. The DNA didn't match. Not only that, but the DNA from the tissue sample belonged to a man. Unless the test was somehow faulty (not likely, as it passed muster with the peer-reviewed *Journal of Forensic Sciences*, in which it was published), Hawley was convicted based on false evidence.

So who did the body belong to? And where did Cora go? It's possible that the body belonged to the victim of another murder, though the more cynical answer is that police planted it there. As for Cora, she may have been murdered and her body disposed of in some other way, or perhaps, as Hawley said, she simply ran away.

Spilsbury went on to become a famous, though controversial, forensic pathologist. One of his most interesting cases was known as the "Brides in the Bath." In the late 1800s and early 1900s, many British men emigrated to America to find their fortunes. By 1910, women in England outnumbered men by 500,000. Women hoping to marry were hard-pressed to find a husband. So Bessie Mundy probably felt lucky when a charming man by the name of Henry Williams proposed to her after only a few weeks of dating. The problem was, his name wasn't Henry, and he was already married to at least five other women. George Joseph Smith—that was his real name—had left his other wives penniless. He would take even more from Bessie.

After they married,

"Brides in the Bath" murderer George Joseph Smith posing with his first murder victim, Bessie Mundy

George asked Bessie to make a will naming him as beneficiary. Bessie had inherited quite a bit of money from her father, a banker. In May of 1912, the couple moved to Herne Bay in the county of Kent on the east coast of England. George had an iron bathtub made for the house and sent his wife to haggle over the price. She would soon die in that tub. George convinced Bessie that she was having seizures and afterward didn't remember them. On July 12, she saw a doctor and described her "symptoms"—really just the things Smith had told her. The next day, George wrote to the same doctor. "Come at once," the note said. "My wife is dead."[4]

The doctor found Bessie drowned in the bathtub, faceup. It appeared to be a horrible accident, but he made note of a strange detail: her right hand was clutching a bar of soap. The coroner's jury found that Bessie had had a seizure and drowned. George buried Bessie in a cheap coffin in a common grave, returned the bathtub, and pocketed his inheritance.

A year later, George married Alice Burnham, a nurse. On their wedding day, he romantically bought a life insurance policy for £500. Two months later, George and Alice vacationed in Blackpool on the northwest coast (as far away from the first murder as possible). As with Bessie, he convinced Alice to see a doctor, this time for headaches. He then made sure to talk to the landlady while his wife was supposedly drowning in the boardinghouse tub. He claimed to have found Alice dead afterward, and no suspicions were raised because no one in Blackpool had heard of Bessie's death. A coroner's jury found that Alice drowned after fainting.

On December 18, 1914, George, under the name of John Lloyd, married Margaret Lofty. They immediately went on a honeymoon in North London. She, too, was "found" by George, drowned in the tub after having visited a doctor the same day for headaches. The death was ruled an accident. But for George, the third time was *not* a charm. Alice Burnham's father read about how Margaret Lofty died and found it eerily similar to his own daughter's death. He shared his suspicions with police, who arrested George in February 1915.

Kent police thought Bessie Mundy's death might also be related. The bodies were exhumed, and Spilsbury conducted the autopsies. With three newlyweds found dead in bathtubs, intentional drowning seemed likely. And the fact that Bessie Mundy was found holding a bar of soap offered a further clue. If she'd had a seizure, it would have slipped out of her hand. She must have died suddenly instead. But if the killer had knocked the women out before drowning them, they should have had head or neck trauma. If he hadn't, the bodies should have shown signs of a fight. Spilsbury found no such suspicious injuries and no signs of poisoning. To find out what happened, Spilsbury did experiments with a "very fine lady swimmer," as he described her.[5] Based on this work, he developed a theory that Smith must have pulled the women's legs sharply up and out of the bath, causing their heads to go underwater. This would have sent water rushing down their throats, putting pressure on the vagus nerves in their necks and slowing their heart rates until the women passed out or died.

Spilsbury testified about this theory in court. Tall, handsome, and well dressed, he had a way of persuading the jury. But in this case, not much persuading was needed, as five of George's surviving wives also testified. One said that he had made her steal, landing her in prison. Three others said he stole their cash, jewelry, and clothing before running off, and a fifth said she thought she was still married to George—he'd lived with her on and off for the past seven years. He was found guilty and hanged in 1915.

Sir Bernard Henry Spilsbury, famed pathologist

The Brides in the Bath case was a bit of a slam dunk. George Smith was an extremely likely suspect in the deaths. After all, what were the chances that three wives would accidentally die in the bathtub, their husband having married them under false pretenses and gaining financially each time? That's to say nothing of the man's five other wives, most of whom he'd robbed penniless. The Crippen case had also seemed cut-and-dried. It was possible that the body belonged to someone else, but unlikely given the fact that Crippen's wife had recently disappeared, and he had lied to her friends about the circumstances and fled the country when police began asking questions. Of course, thanks to DNA, we now know that Crippen may have run off when he saw the writing on the wall: he was about to go down for a crime he didn't commit.

In cases that were less certain at the time, Spilsbury often came under fire. Several times, the public accused him of basing his testimony not on science but on his own assumptions. In 1925, twenty-five-year-old Norman Thorne was accused of killing his girl-friend, Elsie Cameron. Her dismembered body was found on his chicken farm. Norman at first told police that Elsie hadn't visited the farm on the day of her disappearance. When her body was found on the property, he changed his story. He said she had come to the farm claiming to be pregnant and demanding that he marry her. They fought, and he left in a huff. He returned to find that she had hanged herself. Thinking he would be accused, Norman panicked. He cut up the body and buried it.

Police digging for evidence in the Elsie Cameron murder

Spilsbury said the autopsy told a different story. He said the neck showed no sign of strangulation. Rather, Elsie appeared to have been beaten to death—probably by a blunt object like a club. Here's where Spilsbury's testimony became strange. He said that although

Elsie had no bruising on the surface of her skin, she had bruising *under* the skin. Defense experts said that this theory was ridiculous. If the victim had been beaten by a club, she would have had more than just bruising under the skin. She would have appeared battered, and her bones and skull would be fractured. Moreover, the defense said that there were, in fact, signs of strangulation from the hanging. They called Spilsbury's autopsy methods outdated, as he relied on the naked eye rather than the microscope. The defense experts said the bruising, less severe than Spilsbury claimed, was probably a result of the body falling to the floor when Thorne cut the rope from which Elsie hanged. They argued that she had died of shock soon after being cut down.

The jury was faced with two competing medical theories. After debating for just half an hour, they found Thorne guilty. But was the verdict really based on scientific evidence, or was it a popularity contest for the pathologists? The defense's pathologists were unknown to the jurors. Spilsbury, on the other hand, was a celebrity. He had been knighted for his work. The judge even referred to him several times during trial as "the greatest living pathologist."[6]

While the jurors seemed to have been taken by Spilsbury, others were skeptical of his findings and outraged at the verdict. Sir Arthur Conan Doyle himself commented on the case, saying that Thorne hadn't been proven guilty "in view of the medical evidence."[7] Before his execution, Thorne wrote in a letter to his father, "Never mind, Dad, don't worry. I am a martyr to Spilsburyism."[8]

At least in the public view, Spilsbury was no longer infallible. And the fact that two teams of pathologists disagreed on the cause of death showed that forensic science itself was fallible. Answers weren't definite. They were up for interpretation and subject to the limitations of the pathologists' knowledge and methods. And those pathologists were only human.

Meanwhile, in America, a system of conducting scientific autopsies was just taking hold. The English coroner system had been brought to America in the 1600s—before Dr. Wakley's campaign to require coroners be doctors, and so well into the twentieth century in America, most coroners were appointed by the mayor and had no scientific training. Coroner and jury would make a cursory examination of the body and haphazardly declare the cause of death. So if, for instance, someone died of a stomach ailment, the coroner, rather than testing the stomach for poison, might assume that the victim had fallen ill. Doctors were sometimes called in for further examination, but autopsies were rare. There was no protocol for when they should be conducted, and victims' families were often against them, believing them to be desecration of the dead. Those autopsies that were performed were nowhere near as thorough as today's, and much less helpful in solving crimes.

By the early 1900s, coroners were falling out of favor in the nation's largest city. The *New York Times* reported that coroners were accepting bribes to lie about official causes of death. That meant that if a loved one committed suicide, the family could pay the coroner to say it was an accident. Coroners were also bilking the city of money. They were paid by the body and so would report more deaths than there really were. In one case, several bodies were found on separate occasions floating in the East River. None were brought to the morgue for autopsy, and it turned out there was only one body, which the coroner was moving to new spots along the river. In this way, he collected $10,000.

Beyond this shady behavior, most coroners simply didn't know what they were doing. This was displayed in the 1900 murder trial of the lawyer Albert Patrick. He was accused of hiring a butler to kill his wealthy client, eighty-four-year-old William Marsh Rice. The coroner's surgeon first testified that the death was natural, but later changed the cause of death to chloroform poisoning. Albert was convicted, but in a later chloroform murder case, the lungs of the victim were found to be completely different from William's lungs at the time of his death. Five hundred physicians and other experts signed a letter urging a new trial. Albert was finally released in 1912.

It was clear that the New York coroner system was ineffective. Massachusetts had developed a medical examiner's office in 1877, but it hadn't taken hold elsewhere. In 1915, New York officials decided to bring the Massachusetts system to New York. Needless to

say, coroners were against the idea. It would mean they'd be out of jobs. They even made the outrageous claim that the medical examiner system was a ploy to funnel more organs into medical schools (because the city would be conducting more autopsies).

Nevertheless, Charles Norris, who had studied cutting-edge forensic pathology in Europe, became the city's first chief medical examiner

Charles Norris, New York's first chief medical examiner

in 1918. Under the new system, all unexplained deaths were referred to the medical examiner's office. Then, if an autopsy was needed, the body was taken to one of the five morgues, in Manhattan, Staten Island, Queens, Brooklyn, or the Bronx. The city's autopsies did, in fact, increase—from about 8 to 20 percent of all bodies examined, for a total of 1,400 autopsies in 1918. And that meant that murders were detected that might otherwise have gone unnoticed.

Many of these murders involved poison. As in Europe, poison deaths in America were rampant. It may be hard to believe today, when poisonings are so rare and shootings so common, but in 1922, New York had 997 poisonings, compared to 237 shootings. At the time, poison was ubiquitous. It was found in makeups and over-the-counter medicines. There were no warning labels or safety caps, so sometimes the poison was taken by mistake. But it was also used as a murder weapon.

For this reason, Norris hired chemist Alexander Gettler to set up a toxicology lab—the first of its kind in America. In cases of possible poisoning, Gettler would examine the body and decide which tests to run. For instance, if the lips or skin appeared blue, it indicated possible cyanide poisoning, because that poison affects the body's ability to process oxygen. Victims of cyanide poisoning also exude an odor of bitter almonds. That's because the nuts, along with many other plants, contain cyanide—a defense mechanism that discourages insects from eating them. (Sweet almonds—the kind we eat as snacks—do not.) To find poison in the body, Gettler ground the stomach wall, distilled the sludge, and tested it for the given poison. Gettler didn't test just bodies of possible victims for poisons; he also ran tests on other corpses to expand his knowledge. For instance, he tested bodies that hadn't been poisoned to see how much poison they contained naturally; the human body contains trace amounts of poisons, and poisons can also be absorbed from the soil when the body is buried.

Alexander Gettler, toxicologist

Gettler became such an expert on poisons that it was difficult for defense attorneys to dispute his findings in court. Gone were the days of chemists being undermined as expert witnesses, as in the clam chowder case or the Hyde murder appeal. Not only was it getting harder to pass a poisoning off as a natural death, it was also harder for a guilty party to get an acquittal if the case went to trial.

In a 1923 case, eighteen-year-old Charles Avery died of an apparent illness. But the police received a tip from neighbors to investigate Charles's sister, Fannie Creighton. Charles had recently moved to

Newark, New Jersey, to live with Fannie, her husband, and their child. The police exhumed the body, and the medical examiner's office found it to have high levels of arsenic. The police learned that Fannie had taken out a life insurance policy on Charles without ever telling him. They also found in her home Fowler's Solution, a cosmetic product that contained arsenic. She and her husband were brought to trial. Their defense attorney didn't argue as to whether arsenic had been found in the body. But he said that Fannie's Fowler's Solution contained so little arsenic that it was unlikely to have killed anyone. It was more likely that Charles had gotten rat poison (which had a higher concentration of arsenic) from the store where he worked. Why? Using the old Styrian defense, the attorney suggested that Charles might have been an arsenic eater. Alternatively, the attorney said, Charles might have killed himself because he was depressed over an unrequited crush. Based on these possibilities, Fannie was acquitted.

But neighbors had also tipped off the police about the death of Fannie's in-laws, who had lived with her husband and her until their mysterious deaths. This was an Essex County case—out of Gettler's jurisdiction. The prosecution's experts found arsenic in the mother-in-law's body, and Fannie was brought to trial for a second time. Gettler was asked by Fannie's defense attorneys to conduct his own examination of the body. He, too, found arsenic. But he had a hunch that the young mother was innocent. What if, he wondered, the chemical he had found wasn't pure arsenic? Fannie's mother-in-law took several medications, one of which contained bismuth. Gettler knew that bismuth melted at a higher temperature than arsenic. When Gettler heated the arsenic to its melting point, only a small amount melted. The rest remained. That meant that what the prosecutors thought was arsenic was mostly bismuth. The amount of arsenic in the body was minute—not enough to have killed the woman. In other words, she hadn't been poisoned, she'd simply taken a medicine that had traces of arsenic in it (common in medications at that time). Gettler convinced jurors that the mother-in-law couldn't have been poisoned, and Fannie was found not guilty. Little did Gettler know that though Fannie was not guilty in this case, she was, in fact a murderer.

In 1935, Ada Applegate died on Long Island. A physician ruled her death a heart attack. But police soon received an anonymous package containing newspaper clips from Fannie Creighton's earlier murder trials. Ada and her husband had recently moved in with the Creighton family in order to split their rent (a common practice during the Great Depression). Having no toxicologist of their own, the Long Island police sent the body to Gettler. He found it riddled with arsenic. Fannie became a suspect, and though she didn't admit to this murder, she told police that she had killed her brother all those years ago. For weeks, she'd served her brother poisoned chocolate pudding in order to collect on his $1,000 life insurance policy. And she did indeed use her Fowler's Solution to do the job. She'd already been found not guilty in the case, and a person acquitted of a crime cannot be prosecuted again, due to a constitutional clause known as double jeopardy. So she had safely gotten away with that murder.

The police were forced to focus on the present case alone. They learned that Ada Applegate's husband, Everett, had a romantic interest in Fannie's fifteen-year-old daughter, Ruth, and that Fannie strangely had encouraged his pursuit. In fact, Fannie hoped that the two would marry so that she would no longer have to support her daughter. Prosecutors argued that Fannie had killed Ada so that the marriage could go forward. They charged Everett with the statutory rape of Ruth and the murder of his wife. Fannie and Everett stood trial, and this time Gettler testified against Fannie. He said that Ada's body contained four times the lethal dose of arsenic and that it was the same type found in the rat poison Fannie had recently purchased. Again, the jury believed Gettler. Fannie and Everett were found guilty and sent to the electric chair.

Fannie Creighton leaving court after being sentenced to death in the electric chair

In other cases, Norris and Gettler were able to prove the innocence of suspects police thought were guilty. One November morning in 1926, a police officer saw a man kicking a bundle into New York Harbor. When the officer questioned the man, he gave a fake name and address. Later, a taxi driver pulled up, asking police why they were talking to Francesco Travia. So that was his real name! The cabdriver also knew his address: 56 Sackett Street—by the loading docks on the harbor. At Francesco's home, police found a bloody scene: a woman's torso with her severed head lying beside it. It belonged to Anna Fredericksen, a neighbor of Francesco's.

According to the memoirs of Dr. M. Edward Marten, the New York City medical examiner in Brooklyn at the time, Francesco readily confessed to the murder: "Yeah yeah! I killed her. I t'rew her arms and legs in de river. I was goin' to t'row de rest of her in tonight."[9] Case closed. Or so police thought.

Then Marten, along with Norris and his chauffeur, Charlie (last name unknown), arrived on the scene. Norris told police he bet they had no cause of death. Police said that of course they had a cause of death; the woman's head had been cut off. Marten said it was Charlie who guessed at the real story. (During his time with Norris, he'd become an amateur sleuth.) He pointed out that the murdered woman's face was cherry red, indicating carbon monoxide poisoning. Lab work indeed showed carbon monoxide—and not the gruesome dissection—to be the cause of death. Her brain also showed signs of intoxication.

Francesco explained what had really happened. He and Anna had been drinking together. The night grew cold, and they shut the windows and lit the stove. At six a.m. he awoke to find Anna dead. Thinking he'd killed her in a state of drunkenness, he tried to hide the evidence by chopping up the body and throwing it in the river.

Even with the medical examiner shedding light on the real cause of death, Travia still stood trial for murder. But his lawyer was able to prove that Anna did die from carbon monoxide poisoning. Some coffee had boiled over on the stove, putting out the flame and allowing gas to fill the apartment. Travia escaped the death penalty for murder but was jailed for mutilating a dead body.

In spite of Norris's keen mind and Gettler's cutting-edge poison detection, some cases still went unsolved. It was one thing to detect poison in a body and another to find the poisoner, especially in a case where there was no clear motive. Seventeen-year-old Lillian Goetz lived at home and worked as a stenographer for a fabric company. On the morning of July 31, 1922, her mother offered to make her a lunch to take to work. "No, mother," Lillian said. "It's too hot to take a heavy lunch with me today. I'll just step out and get a light sandwich and some pie."[10]

People often recall, after a tragedy, how a simple decision saved them from the fates of the victims. In this case, the opposite was true. Lillian did grab a sandwich and slice of pie on her lunch break—at the Shelburne Restaurant on Broadway between Twenty-Fifth and Twenty-Sixth Streets. On returning to work, she became sick to her stomach and was sent home in a taxi. She wasn't the only one. Ambulances were arriving all over the neighborhood as more than fifty pie eaters fell ill.

Earlier in the day, restaurant patrons had complained that the huckleberry and blackberry pies had burned their throats. Hearing this, the owner of the Shelburne, Samuel Drexler, asked his brother-in-law to try a piece. He did and assured Drexler that the pie was fine. Later, the brother-in-law suffered from intense stomach pain, and a physician pumped his stomach, saving his life. Once Drexler saw that the pies really were making people sick, he ordered that no more be sold. He also sent samples to a chemist, who said there was arsenic in the crust. It wasn't just the huckleberry and blueberry pies that were poisoned, but all the pies and other pastries, too.

Though many patrons were poisoned, few actually died. Norris, the medical examiner in the case, said that the high dose of poison in the pie had caused the pie eaters to violently vomit, purging the poison from their systems so that they survived. Lillian was not so lucky. Though she seemed to be recovering that evening, by four a.m. she had again become ill. A physician was unable to save her, and she died with her mother by her side, one of six murder victims.

The investigation began. Accidental poisoning was ruled out. The owners didn't keep rat poison on hand, and the pie ingredients were tested and found to be pure. While all employees had access to the refrigerator where the dough was kept, and even an outsider could have grabbed it, that wasn't likely. The arsenic was found throughout the dough, suggesting that it had been mixed well, probably in the bakery.

Louis Mandel was the head baker on Monday, his first day back to work since he'd left the restaurant several weeks earlier to start his own business. When that didn't pan out, he returned to his old position. He told investigators that when he arrived in the morning, there were five pounds of dough in the refrigerator left over from Saturday. His assistant, Louis Freedman, mixed two more pounds in order to have seven pounds total for the day's baking. The Monday dough was analyzed and found free of poison. It was the Saturday dough that was tainted.

Saturday had been the last day of work for the previous baker, Charles Abramson. He had given his notice a few days earlier, fearing that he would soon be laid off when Louis M. was given his old job back. Charles said that Louis F.—his assistant, too—had mixed the dough, but Louis F. denied this. Either had the opportunity. But who had the motive?

The impending layoff seemed a possible motive for Charles. He told investigators that on Saturday, he had been feeling bitter toward his boss. Then, when Charles returned to the restaurant the morning of the poisoned pie incident, Drexler said he'd never planned on firing Charles in the first place. So by Monday, Charles was no longer mad. Of course, the dough had been mixed on Saturday. But after questioning Charles, district attorney Joab Banton was convinced of his innocence. Things hadn't turned out badly for Charles. He'd already found a new job that paid better than the Shelburne.

Both Charles and Louis F. were suspects, but Banton repeatedly told reporters that there wasn't enough evidence to arrest either man. Moreover, neither had a strong motive to poison the customers. In fact, no one did. It seemed likely that the killing was about bloodlust—the desire to kill people. In 1916, there had been a mass poisoning at a Chicago banquet for the archbishop. Several diners became violently ill, and the soup was found to be laced with arsenic. Police searched the apartment of Jean Crones, a cook, and found poison there. But Crones himself was never found. In the poisoned pie case, police had no such clues that led to Charles, Louis F., or anyone else.

Killings by strangers are difficult to solve because the police ordinarily rely on leads generated by interviewing the victims' friends, family, and acquaintances. They also consider motive, narrowing the pool of suspects. If the killer didn't know his or her victims and had no reason to kill them, then both trails are dead ends. As Banton told reporters: "This is a most baffling case, and may require a Sherlock Holmes to solve it, although on the other hand, it may have a simple explanation."[11] It turned out the first option was true: the case was never solved.

Thankfully, the era of rampant poisonings was coming to a close. Authorities had clamped down on the sale of products containing poison. Medical examiners were better able to detect poisoning. And juries were finding expert testimony against poisoners to be more and more reliable. However, the decrease in poisonings didn't mean there were fewer murders. As the population in New York grew, so did the number of bodies examined by medical examiners. By the 1930s, each borough morgue was handling about eight autopsies a day.

One of those bodies came in piece by piece. In 1931, a salesman driving across a bridge saw what he thought was a ham lying in the road. He pulled closer to get a better look. It was a human thigh. He called over a policeman, who confirmed the gruesome find. The thigh was brought to the Brooklyn morgue, where Dr. Marten examined it. He found on it a clean cut through the hip and knee joints and theorized that it might have been severed by a doctor. Perhaps it was a cadaver limb placed on the bridge as a medical-student prank. But Gettler did a toxicology report and found neither the preservative used on cadavers nor any of the anesthetics used during operations.

Marten found it extremely unlikely that in that day and age an amputation would be performed without anesthesia and that the amputated limb would somehow wind up on a bridge. It was also unlikely that someone would cut a thigh off a dead body after a natural death, and again, that the thigh would wind up on a bridge. It was far more likely that the thigh belonged to a murder victim, but who?

A Brooklyn newspaper dated six days before the discovery was wrapped around the thigh. That gave police a likely time of death. Now Marten set about determining the identity of the victim. Because a woman's body is evolutionarily adapted to bear children, her pelvis and thighs are different from a man's. By measuring the angle of the thighbone in relation to the hip socket, Marten determined that the thigh belonged to a man. He then took X-rays to determine the calcification of the bones. From this, he could tell that the man was older than twenty-five. The length of the thighbone suggested that the man was shorter than average—five feet, four inches tall. Based on the size of the thigh, Marten believed the man to be extremely stocky, weighing about 200 pounds. The thigh had an odor of alcohol, and toxicology reports confirmed that the man had been drunk when he died. The hairs on the thigh were light brown, and it was likely the hair on the man's head would be the same color. The man had fair skin.

Marten had learned quite a bit about the victim just from his thigh. Three days after the thigh was found, investigators had a bit of luck. Part of a chest, with the same blood type, hair, skin, and build, turned up in a Brooklyn lumberyard. The following day, the right thigh, left lower leg, and parts of the right and left arms were found, and a couple days later, a hip. By now, the newspapers had gotten ahold of the case and the whole city was looking for body parts. Finally, the head, along with two feet, two forearms, and two hands, were found by a gardener digging up topsoil in a vacant lot. The head had a jagged hole, showing that the murder weapon was likely an ax or hatchet.

Marten now had much of the corpse but still didn't know the man's name. He had had no dental work and bore no tattoos, both of which are helpful for determining identity. A dirty shirt was found with the body—and the bloodstains were of the same blood type as the body parts. Once washed, the shirt proved to be a valuable clue. A laundry mark was visible on the collar.

In those days, men wore button-down shirts every day and had them cleaned at laundries. The laundries marked the shirts with permanent ink so that they could be returned to the correct owners. Different laundries had different systems of marking, so one might read W-K33 and another, H 8421-3-5. These marks were helpful in identifying bodies and solving crimes. The first of the above marks, for instance, was found on bloody towels connected to the murder of a jewelry salesman. The police located the laundry, and a worker there identified the customer. That customer turned out to be the killer. These laundry marks were so helpful in solving crimes that some police departments had files of laundry marks used by all the laundries in the city.

Laundry mark on a shirt, similar to the one used to solve the Brooklyn Butcher case

In this case, the police searched the laundries until they found the right one, which was located in the Greenpoint neighborhood of Brooklyn. The laundryman supplied the name and address of the owner of the shirt. Police found that man, a bootlegger and owner of a speakeasy, at home. But he said the shirt didn't belong to him. It belonged to his ex-partner, Andrew Zubresky. The man was so cheap that he would sneak his shirts into his friends' laundry bags so that he didn't have to pay for his own cleaning. Zubresky and the owner of the laundry bag had had a falling out, and Zubresky was now running a different speakeasy. At that location, the police found Zubresky's wife (identified by Marten only as Mrs. Andrew Zubresky). She said that she and her husband had argued. He'd withdrawn $1,400 from his bank account and gone to Europe. Her description of her husband matched the one Marten had made based only on the thigh.

Police didn't believe Mrs. Zubresky's story. If her husband had taken a European holiday, then why had he wound up all over Brooklyn? Heightening their suspicions, they learned that the Zubreskys had been tried for the murder of Mrs. Zubresky's first husband in Cleveland. He, too, had owned a speakeasy where Zubresky was the bartender. Had Mrs. Zubresky offed her first and second husbands? Detectives interrogated her, but she never broke.

When the police followed Mrs. Zubresky, they saw that she was living with Charles Obreitis, a butcher-turned-bartender in the Zubreskys' Greenpoint speakeasy. He confessed to the murder. Obreitis said Mrs. Zubresky had asked him to kill her husband, promising money and romance. Obreitis had agreed. One night, he got Zubresky drunk and hit him over the head with a hatchet. Then he was faced with the problem of getting rid of the body. He decided to cut it up (using his butcher skills) and deposit the parts all over Brooklyn, apparently thinking police wouldn't figure out that they belonged to the same person. Which poses the question: exactly how many people's body parts did he think they would suppose were lying around the city?

The final step in solving the murder was to prove without a doubt that the body belonged to Zubresky. As a veteran of the US Army, his fingerprints were on file in Washington, DC. But since the body had been left in the open air, most of the fingers had rotted away.

The right thumb was intact, but mummified. Marten tried everything to get a thumbprint, to no avail. Finally, he went on vacation, preserving the thumb in a glycerin-formaldehyde solution. When he came back, the thumb had unexpectedly plumped up. He got a print from it and it matched perfectly the one from the War Department. Obreitis went to prison for twenty years. Mrs. Zubresky stuck to her story and walked free, but she was later jailed for forging Zubresky's checks.

In another case, the medical examiner had a hunch as to the identity of a body but needed to prove it without a doubt. Call it the Case of the Party Food. Jennie Becker was fed up with her husband's cheating ways—he was married with three children, for goodness' sake. It was time to stop fooling around. But Becker had no intention of being faithful to his wife. Frankly, he'd fallen out of love with her. This might have been just another unhappy marriage. But Abraham Becker was a bad man. And he came up with a bad plan.

On April 6, 1922, Abraham and Jennie went to a party thrown by their friends the Linders. Abraham doted on Jennie at the party, but it was all a ruse. On the drive home, he claimed they were having car trouble. His friend Reuben Norkin was standing on a street corner nearby. Abraham picked his buddy up, explaining to Jennie that perhaps Reuben would know how to fix the car. If something seemed off to Jennie or if she protested in some way, she nevertheless ended up with the men in an empty lot. There, Abraham popped the trunk and said, "Come here, and I'll show you what's the matter."[12] Jennie leaned over the hood to see. Then Abraham hit her with an iron bar. Reuben had been part of the plan all along and stood lookout while Abraham buried his wife.

Afterward, Abraham told his suspicious neighbors that Jennie had gone to Philadelphia and even showed them a telegram that said,

EVERYTHING OK WITH ME
LETTER WILL FOLLOW JENNIE.[13]

As promised, a letter did follow, which read:

Dear Husband Abe:

This is to inform you that I have gone away with another man who I was married to before I married you. He said he would arrest me for bigamy if I didn't go with him. I hope you will be a better father than I have been a mother. I remain your ungrateful wife, Jennie.[14]

Abraham was laying it on a bit thick. But the letter was post-marked from Philadelphia, and so the neighbors believed that it was from Jennie—for a while.

Several months later, a badly decomposed body was found, and the neighbors got to talking again. Could it be Jennie? Police heard the gossip and brought "Husband Abe" to the morgue.

Ever the charming husband, he said, "It don't look like my wife. Jennie was a bigger woman."[15]

It wasn't so much his words as his nonchalant attitude that convinced police of Abraham's guilt. They even found a man who said that Abraham had asked him to send the telegram and letter from Philadelphia. But how could they be sure the body was Jennie's? The body's clothing had no laundry marks, and dental records were unavailable. In the end it was a familiar name—Dr. Gettler—who cracked the case based on the contents of the stomach. Whoever this was had had a somewhat unusual dinner prior to dying. Gettler found traces of oranges, raisins, cherries, and almonds. Police asked the Linders what they had served at their party. Sure enough, oranges, raisins, cherries, and almonds were all on the menu. Reuben confessed to everything, but not Abraham. Nonetheless, both men were convicted and sent to the electric chair.

Not every case cracked by the New York Medical Examiner's Office was based on the autopsy alone. "Tour men," medical examiners deployed to the scenes of unexplained deaths, gathered clues from the crime scene, too. Medical examiners still "tour" crime scenes today, the purpose being to view the context of the death and determine whether a crime occurred. The importance of these visits is apparent in a 1920s case involving a missing key.

Boardinghouses were common during the 1920s and '30s. People would rent bedrooms upstairs and share the eating and living space downstairs. Typically room and "board"—meals—were provided, as well as cleaning services. Boardinghouses could be rather genteel—Sherlock Holmes and Watson stayed in such a home. They could also be cheap, providing affordable housing for the poor. In one such lower-rent boardinghouse, a chambermaid knocked on the door of an elderly woman and, getting no response, unlocked it. She found the woman dead in her bed. Though the old woman lived in a communal home, she was a lonely person. She had just one friend, the middle-aged man across the hall. The boarders were impressed at how kind he was to her.

The police arrived and, seeing no injuries, assumed the woman had died of natural causes. Still, they followed the protocol of calling the medical examiner, and it was a good thing they did. The medical examiner found something amiss. If the chambermaid had to unlock the door to let herself in, then the door must have been locked. But if the old woman herself had locked it, then where was the key? The chambermaid didn't know, and the police couldn't find it. They thought to check with her one friend—and found it in his pocket. That discovery led to an autopsy of the woman, during which the medical examiner found signs of strangulation. The neighbor confessed. He had been sneaking around the woman's apartment looking for money. When she caught him, he killed her. As it turned out, her one friend in the world was also her worst enemy. As to why he locked the door from the outside, he told the police it seemed like a good idea at the time. Well, it wasn't his worst idea that day.

Cases like these made the New York Medical Examiner's Office an example to other cities, counties, and states. Throughout the 1900s, coroners gave way to medical examiners. Meanwhile, detectives took the place of coroners when it came to investigating crime scenes and interviewing witnesses.

DEADLY DOLLHOUSES

Frances Glessner Lee influenced crime scene investigations in a big way—through miniatures. A fan of Sherlock Holmes, Lee one day asked her brother's friend George Burgess Magrath about his work in the Massachusetts Medical Examiner's Office. The conversation blossomed into a lifelong friendship, and Lee loved hearing about her friend's investigations.

Magrath would often say that there weren't enough people being trained in crime detection. A wealthy woman, Lee had the means to fix that. In 1931, she donated money to establish the Harvard Department of Legal Medicine, where crime-solving seminars were held for medical examiners, lawyers, detectives, state troopers, coroners, insurance men, and newspaper reporters.

Next, Lee embarked on an unusual project that would help investigators find clues at crime scenes. She created a series of twenty dollhouse scenes, which she called the Nutshell Studies of Unexplained Death. For research, she read the newspaper, visited active crime scenes, talked to investigators, and attended autopsies. Then she created the fictional but "ripped from the headlines" scenes. One that may have been inspired by the Brides in the Bath case featured a woman in the bathtub. Unlike in the Brides in the Bath, however, this woman appeared to have gone out partying with her friends. Was the death an accident or murder?

Each dollhouse cost about as much as building an actual house. A carpenter constructed the home on a one-inch-to-one-foot scale, complete with working doors and keys. Meanwhile, Lee made each doll by hand, painting their faces, sewing matching outfits, and knitting sweaters. Sometimes she created toys for the doll children, including a miniature dollhouse inside one dollhouse. After all that loving handiwork, she would kill the doll, stabbing her, tying a noose around his neck, etc. Finally, she would place clues at the scene—miniature bullet shells, rolled-up cigarettes, and more. Now it no longer looked like a child's toy—more like a nightmare.

Dollhouse crime scenes from Frances Glessner Lee's
Nutshell Studies of Unexplained Death

Students at the Harvard seminars would study the scenes for a day. Lee encouraged them to examine the scene in clockwise fashion, leaving no stone unturned. In one scene, a woman appeared to have committed suicide, but at the house, there was a fresh-baked cake, newly washed clothing, and a freshly filled ice cube tray—hardly the marks of a suicidal woman (as any TV mystery fan knows). After taking notes, the students would try to reconstruct the crime. Students said that this exercise really did help them handle challenging cases in the field. The nutshells now belong to the Baltimore Office of the Medical Examiner and are still used for teaching seminars. And for any retro TV mystery fans, Lee was the inspiration for Jessica Fletcher in *Murder, She Wrote*.

3

Elementary, My Dear Watson: The First Detectives

For hundreds of years, coroners led the charge in solving murders—as best they could, anyway. During this time, police officers patrolled the streets and chased down any criminals caught in the act. But if a crime occurred out of sight, police had little recourse. Then, around 1800, the modern world's first detective came on the scene. His name was François Eugène Vidocq, and he came from an unlikely place: prison. Vidocq was a wild young man, by his own accounts. He stole, fought, and had numerous girlfriends. When he found one amour, Francine, dining at a tavern with another man, he "heartily thumped the astonished pair,"[1] according to his memoirs. Francine fled the scene, but the soldier stayed and pressed charges. Vidocq was jailed for three months for the attack, a sentence that would be parlayed into years in prison and on the run.

By some accounts, Vidocq's troubles worsened when he forged a pardon for a fellow inmate who had stolen grain to feed his starving family. However, according to Vidocq's memoirs, his crime was less heroic and actually a complete misunderstanding. The fellow inmate had stolen not grain, but garden tools to work his small farm. And he was apparently not starving, for he had promised any prisoner 100 crowns if they got him released. Vidocq's friends began forging a note of pardon, working in Vidocq's cell because it was quiet there. The prisoner was released, but afterward the forgery was discovered. The thief was captured and blamed Vidocq's friends and Vidocq himself. Vidocq always maintained that he was innocent of this. Whether that's true is unknown. It was the crime that initiated his outlaw status, so to admit to it in his memoirs could have meant a return to prison. At any rate, he was judged guilty. To avoid being transferred to a harsher prison, Vidocq escaped—for the first of many times—by dressing as a guard.

He was ultimately caught and sentenced to eight years in the Bagne, the very type of prison he feared. Here, prisoners wore arm and leg chains while doing heavy labor—and even while sleeping. Many died before they could complete their prison sentences. Vidocq became a slave laborer on the chain gang. Eventually, Vidocq escaped the lockup, but he remained on the run for the rest

François Eugène Vidocq, the world's first detective

of his life. He would float from town to town, doing honest work, only to be discovered again as an escaped convict. (If you are a literature or musical theater fan and this is all starting to sound familiar, it's because Vidocq later became friends with Victor Hugo, and Hugo based the character of Jean Valjean in his novel *Les Misérables* on Vidocq.)

Because of his repeated prison escapes, Vidocq became an outlaw hero. But Vidocq wasn't that kind of criminal—not really. Rather, he was a man still paying for what was supposed to be a short jail sentence. So when a band of robbers asked him to join them in their escapades, he said no, and for that, they turned him in to the Lyons police. Vidocq turned the tables on the thieves, however, contacting the head of police and offering to help him arrest the crooks in exchange for his own freedom. And that's how Vidocq wound up on the other side of the law.

By 1809, Vidocq had made his way to Paris. With Napoleon conquering most of Europe, the nation's capital had become an international hub. The population was fast approaching the one million mark, and crime was rampant. With an estimated 5,000 pickpockets and a murder every hour, the police were outnumbered by criminals. Wealthy people went out with armed guards, and even the middle class hired security guards to protect their homes from burglars.

In this milieu, Vidocq's profile as a police informer rose. As the story goes, Empress Josephine (the wife of Napoleon) had an emerald necklace that was stolen. Vidocq offered to find it for the police. By asking around in his criminal network, Vidocq located the necklace within three days. Soon, he was investigating major crimes as Paris's first undercover detective. After many successes, he convinced the police to let him create his own bureau—with ex-convicts as his detectives. After all, they knew the criminals, and the criminals knew who committed the crimes. In 1817, Vidocq and his twelve agents made 772 arrests—fifteen of those for murder. The bureau, called Le Brigade de Sûreté (the security brigade), acted in all twenty-four districts of Paris. Over time, it became the Sûreté Nationale, a national detective bureau that predated the FBI.

Vidocq saw the benefits of a diverse squad of detectives. By 1818, he was employing women detectives—years before other police forces followed suit. Decades later, Kate Warne became the first female private investigator in America, solving several murders on behalf of the Pinkerton Detective Agency and helping to thwart an assassination attempt on President Lincoln. Women detectives didn't join Scotland Yard until 1933, at which point they focused on high-society crime, drug trafficking, human trafficking, and female crime bosses. They were heralded by an Associated Press article: "Unmarried, athletic and shrewd, the three new operatives of the feminine sex are as much at home wearing evening gowns at a night club as masquerading in disguises befitting the sordid underworld."[2]

The female Sûreté detectives, like their male counterparts, had criminal records, allowing them to move with ease through the underworld. One was nicknamed the Nun. She'd gone to prison at the age of twelve for stealing and spent most of her young life there (where she gained a reputation for modesty that earned her the moniker). Then, in her late twenties, she put her skills to better use. She was Vidocq's expert on burglaries and caught many thieves. She had, as Vidocq put it, the gift of the gab, which led to people telling her all sorts of things in the course of her investigations. The

Kate Warne, the first female detective in the United States (standing center)

Sûreté's women detectives became the focus of many crime novels. And Vidocq himself was the model for Edgar Allan Poe's popular detective Auguste Dupin, along with many other heroes of the page. In fact, Vidocq's life was so often fictionalized (some say by Vidocq himself) that it can be difficult to separate the man from the legend.

French writer Alexandre Dumas recorded a story in which Vidocq used firearm analysis to solve the high-profile murder of the Comtesse Isabelle d'Arcy in 1822. If true, it puts Vidocq ahead of his time not just in detective work, but in forensic science, too. Isabelle's much older husband, Comte d'Arcy, was accused of shooting her to death. His motive: Isabelle was seeing another man. Vidocq didn't think the count was the murdering type, but would the evidence match his hunch? At the time, medical students were performing autopsies as part of their training, but the public frowned upon any such interference with the dead. So Vidocq acted in secret, asking a doctor to remove the bullet from the head wound. The detective then compared the bullet to the comte's dueling pistols. It fit neither. Next, Vidocq investigated the comtesse's amour, a man known as Deloro. The detective hired an actress to feign interest in Deloro so that she could enter his apartment. There, the comtesse's jewelry was found, along with a pistol that matched the bullet. It was Deloro, not the comte, who committed the murder.

Though Vidocq may have used forensic science, he was primarily a detective. For the first modern forensic scientist, we'll look to England—but not Scotland Yard. Scotland Yard, so named either because it was the site of a residence that once housed visiting Scottish royalty or because the back entrance opened onto a street called Great Scotland Yard (named for a man named Scott), was headquarters for the London Metro Police and is still a commonly used name for the police force. It was founded in 1829 and deployed its first plainclothes detectives in 1842. While some Londoners viewed these secretive police officers as spies, popular British writers saw them as heroes. Charles Dickens based the kind but tenacious Inspector Bucket from *Bleak House* on a Scotland Yard detective. And real-life detective Richard Tanner became a darling of the British press when he solved Britain's first train murder.

On July 9, 1864, two men entered a railway car and found it splattered in blood. Soon after, the engineer of another train saw a man lying on the tracks. It was sixty-nine-year-old Thomas Briggs, a banker. Unconscious and badly wounded, he died the next night. The murderer had apparently robbed Briggs of his gold watch and chain and a pair of glasses and then thrown the man off the train. Before fleeing the scene, the robber made a crucial mistake. He put on the victim's hat and left his own behind. Before mass production, something like a hat could be traced to its maker. In this case, the address of the hat maker was inscribed inside. The shop was located in the Marylebone neighborhood of London. If Detective Tanner could link the hat maker to the hat owner, he would find the murderer.

Scotland Yard asked the public for information regarding the hat and the stolen watch and chain. A jeweler, rather thematically named John Death, told police that a German man had come into his shop and exchanged the dead man's chain for something else. A cabdriver then provided the next clue. A family friend, Franz Muller, had brought a small cardboard box—bearing the jeweler's name—to the man's home and given it to one of the children. Franz had been engaged to the cabdriver's oldest daughter but had left London for New York on July 15. The cabdriver also explained that he had bought the Marylebone hat found on the train and given it to Franz as a gift. The cabdriver gave police a photo of Franz, and Death confirmed that he was the same man who had traded the gold chain. Though Franz was en route to America, Tanner caught up with him and found that the robber still had the missing watch and hat. He was busted.

It was gumshoe detective work at its best, but not exactly forensic science. Soon Londoners, and people around the world, were reading about a different kind of detective—one based not on the real-life investigators of Scotland Yard but on the imaginings of Sir Arthur Conan Doyle. Doyle published his first Sherlock Holmes story, *A Study in Scarlet*, in 1887. In it, Dr. John Watson is in London recuperating from a war injury and seeking a roommate. A friend introduces him to Sherlock Holmes at his place of employment: a hospital chemistry lab. Watson describes the strange things Holmes does in the lab. For one thing, Holmes announces that he has discovered an "infallible test for blood stains . . . old or new."[3] (This was before such a test was available to police.) He also warns Watson that he works with strong poisons. Watson's friend adds that he once saw Holmes beating a cadaver in the hospital dissecting room to see how bruises form after death.

Back at their shared apartment, Watson describes Holmes's knowledge base. He knows nothing of literature, philosophy, or astronomy—not even that the Earth revolves around the sun! But he is well versed in chemistry, anatomy, British law, poisons, the different soils of London, and "every detail of every horror perpetrated in the century."[4] Who would have such interests as these? A forensic scientist, of course.

Illustration of Sherlock Holmes from the first edition of Sir Arthur Conan Doyle's *A Study in Scarlet*

When Scotland Yard asks Holmes to help solve a murder, we see what a specialist he really is. From this point, the story reads like an episode of *CSI: Victorian London*. Holmes uses a tape measure and magnifying glass to examine the crime scene, explaining to Watson, "They say that genius is an infinite capacity for taking pains. . . . It's a very bad definition, but it does apply to detective work."[5]

Holmes then smells the lips of the victim, Enoch J. Drebber—and detects poison. He even does a bit of handwriting analysis. "Rache" has been written on the wall in blood. Scotland Yard thinks the killer had begun writing *Rachel* but was interrupted. Holmes, however, knows that *Rache* means revenge in German. But the letters are not written in the way Germans form letters. So that clue was meant to throw detectives off track.

Outside, Holmes observes wheel marks and foot impressions and deduces that two men arrived in a cab, one tall and the other well dressed—the victim, Drebber. Because hoof marks show that the horses wandered aimlessly, he knows that one of the men who went inside was the cabdriver. He even judges by the ashes left at the scene that the man smokes Trichinopoly cigars (he's done a study on this, and at this point, the reader would expect no less).

As Holmes solves the crime (which was indeed done for *Rache*), Holmes explains to Watson that whereas most people think forward, detectives must think backward. If *x* happened, then what had to have happened before it? "There's the scarlet thread of murder running through the colourless skein of life," he says. "Our duty is to unravel it, and isolate it, and expose every inch of it."[6]

Unlike most crime-novel sleuths of the day, Holmes was based not on a real-life detective but on a doctor. Sir Arthur Conan Doyle attended medical school at the University of Edinburgh, where he was an assistant to Professor Joseph Bell. Bell used deductive reasoning to diagnose patients. He could also tell a person's profession just by looking at them. For instance, a woman holding a vial came to see him, and he knew before speaking to her that her husband was a tailor. Bell explained that the vial was stopped with the papers around which tailors typically wound their threads. He could also guess where in the city a person had been based on the mud on their shoes. Bell inspired Doyle to write about a different kind of detective. He said, "If he [Bell] were a detective, he would surely reduce this fascinating but unorganized business to something nearer an exact science. I would try if I could get this effect."[7]

In the Sherlock Holmes stories, Doyle went beyond describing the work of real-life detectives. He predicted the type of work they would do in the future. Some of the first forensic scientists said that their work was inspired by Sherlock Holmes. One such man was Edmond Locard, who opened the world's first crime lab and was known as the French Sherlock Holmes. His focus was on crime scene evidence.

4

Not without a Trace: The Introduction of Crime Scene Evidence

While Sherlock Holmes was solving murder cases on the page, Hans Gross was prosecuting criminals in Austria. But it was Gross's manual for police officers that would live on in history. In 1893, he wrote the book *Criminal Investigation: A Practical Textbook for Magistrates, Police Officers, and Lawyers.* It was groundbreaking, providing for the first time step-by-step instructions for conducting crime scene investigations. In a way, many of the TV-mystery story lines owe themselves to Gross. For instance, he writes that the investigating officer should secure the perimeter of the scene and preserve all evidence. Then the officer should take notes, realizing that even the smallest observations may be important.

"The zealous Investigating Officer will note on his walks the footprints found on the dust of the highway," Gross writes. "He will observe the tracks of animals, of the wheels of carriages, the marks of pressure on the grass where someone has sat or lain down, or perhaps deposited a burden. He will examine little pieces of paper that have been thrown away, marks or injuries on trees, displaced stones, broken glass or pottery, doors and windows open or shut in an unusual manner. Every thing will afford an opportunity for drawing conclusions and explaining what must have previously taken place."[1]

Murder in the House (1890) by Jakub Schikaneder

Gross encourages the officer to keep an open mind, even if he has been told what happened. He describes a case in which two men, whom he calls Sp. and B., encouraged an old man, T., to walk with them to a cattle market one autumn. The next day, T. was found beaten and unconscious. He came to and told police what little he remembered. The morning of the attack, he, Sp., and B. had set out for the market and stopped by the roadside for lunch in the afternoon. They rested until around three p.m.—he was certain of the time because he had heard church bells ringing—and then continued on. About an hour later, Sp. and B. said they wondered if the market would be closed because of a cattle plague. Perhaps they should ask in a nearby village. But T. said they had no reason to believe that the market was closed, and anyway, they could ask at an inn along the road. They would have more updated information than the villagers.

But Sp. and B. insisted on going to the village, and so T. said to go without him. (Walking was hard for him, and he didn't want to make the extra trip.) He would continue walking, and they could catch up with him later. After walking for a while, T. sat down on a milestone to wait. It was then that he felt a blow to his head from behind and blacked out. He was found unconscious, his money to purchase cattle gone. T. died several days later, and investigators suspected that Sp. and B. had killed him. They guessed that Sp. and B. knew that T. wouldn't make the extra trip and had used the ruse of the detour to plan their attack and sneak up on him.

The men insisted that they really had gone into the town to ask about the market. They had looked for T. along the road but couldn't find him. Sp. and B. said it was dark by the time they passed the spot where T. was found, and so they didn't see him lying in the ditch. Sp. and B. had continued to the market without T. and only learned of his attack on the way back, when a peasant asked them to come to his house to identify the poor man. Villagers confirmed that the men had been in town and that it would be impossible to make the trip from point A (where they had stopped for lunch) to point B (the town) and finally to point C (where T. was found unconscious) before dark if they'd left at three p.m. Still, police prosecuted Sp. and B, and they were convicted.

The next spring, however, the men appealed the case, pointing a finger at a young man with a bad reputation who'd been hanging around the neighborhood at the time. The appeal hinged on whether the men would have seen the unconscious T. lying beside the road. The townspeople said it would have been too dark. So perhaps Sp. and B. were telling the truth. Police arrested the other young man instead. But the investigating officer decided to see for himself whether it would have been too dark to see. He asked two astronomers which day that spring would mirror the same day in the fall that the crime took place. On that day, he set out along the road at three p.m. and took the detour into town. He lingered there for a while and then returned to the spot on the road where T. had been killed. It was still light out. He then walked along the road many times to see if the ditch was ever out of sight. It wasn't. Finally, night fell, and the lights went out on the possibility of Sp.'s and B.'s innocence.

Reading Gross's advice, you can't help but imagine that he would have launched a different kind of investigation in the Wyoming barroom shooting of Charles Davis. Sure, three witnesses said they saw Signor act in self-defense. But what if those witnesses were just saying that because they were friends with Signor? That's not to say that their testimonies should be dismissed. But the evidence has to be examined, too. And at the time that Gross wrote his manual, that part of murder investigations was lacking.

Besides thoroughness on the part of police, Gross urged the use of forensic science experts in murder cases. He said toxicologists, botanists, chemists, and handwriting and firearm experts should all be called on when needed. In particular, microscopists should examine the evidence left behind. The idea wasn't unheard of. As far back as 1847, the microscope was used to solve the murder of the French Duchess of Choiseul-Praslin, Fanny Sebastiani.

Early one morning, Fanny's servants heard crashing and screaming and ran to their mistress's room to investigate. Minutes later, they were joined by Fanny's husband, who claimed to have come running, like the servants, when he heard the commotion. He soon became a suspect, after investigators learned of the couple's unhappy marriage.

The duke, Charles Laure Hugo Theobald, employed a governess, Henriette Deluzy-Desportes, to care for the couple's nine children. At the trial, Henriette explained that the duchess didn't like spending time with the children, preferring to be by herself. That left Henriette and the duke to walk in the gardens with the children and relax as a family together in the playroom.

Fanny's diary entries and letters to her husband told a different story: that the governess had essentially moved into the house—and along with the duke was keeping the children away from the duchess, who was now relegated to her bedroom quarters. Fanny asked that the governess be dismissed so that Fanny could care for her own children. Barring that, she asked to be allowed to travel to escape the troubling situation.

In an undated letter to the duke, Fanny wrote, "You are, doubtless, free to do what suits you; but you are not free to have my daughters brought up by a person whom I despise as her shameful conduct deserves. For a long time I have sought an explanation with you; I have done what I could to obtain it, but you refuse it. I demand, then, that you authorize me to travel, to avoid greater scandals. During that time you will reflect on the course it will be suitable for you to adopt. The day will come, Theobald, when you will return to yourself, and will perceive how unjust and cruel you have been to the mother of your children, in order to please a crack-brain who respects nothing."[2] The crack-brain she referred to was, of course, Henriette.

Fanny's primary beef with Henriette seems to have been that she had usurped her role as mother to the children. But rumors were spreading that Henriette wasn't just hogging the children, but snogging the husband, too. Fanny's family got involved, and finally, the duke was forced to dismiss Henriette. She did not go willingly. Afterward, she wrote letters to the children proclaiming her motherly love for them and asking, by the way, how their father was holding up. She also mentioned that she wished she were dead—so badly did she miss them. The children genuinely loved their governess and hated that she had been sent away. So the rift between mother and children continued.

Though she pined for the duke and his children, Henriette did wish to go on with her life. She'd been offered a job at a school, but only if she could prove that the rumored affair never happened. For that, she needed a letter of recommendation from the duchess. The duke told Henriette to come by the house to pick up the letter on August 18. But by that date, the letter hadn't been written yet—and never would be. Because that was the morning Fanny was found dead.

The duke first told investigators that he had entered Fanny's room only after the servants. But when police found the duke's bloody pistol under a sofa in Fanny's room, he was forced to change his story. Now he said that he had arrived at the scene before the servants, carrying his pistol to fight off an intruder. Seeing Fanny lying in a pool of blood, he dropped the pistol and cradled his wife. Since she couldn't be helped, he went back to his room to wash up, only to return to the scene once the servants arrived. People may lie, but pistols don't. Under a microscope, pathologist Auguste Ambroise Tardieu found hair and skin tissue on the gun. It had clearly been used to beat the duchess. Police theorized that that morning, Theobald had asked Fanny to write the letter. She had refused, and he'd flown into a rage, killing her. The duke was convicted, but he poisoned himself before he could be sent to prison. Or, if you believe the conspiracy theorists of the day, he faked his own death and escaped with the help of the royal family.

Edmond Locard, founder of the world's first crime laboratory

Though France was a leader in forensic science, even there, its use was neither widespread nor consistent. Edmond Locard hoped to change that. He had been a student of Alexandre Lacassagne, but rather than focusing on the body, Locard turned his attention to the crime scene. Sherlock Holmes could tell where in London a person had been by glancing at the mud on his shoes. Locard knew that examining evidence wasn't as simple as that. But he was inspired by Holmes to scientifically investigate such things. In one case, Locard was able to prove that a man had visited a flour mill by examining the mud on his shoes, which included a layer of flour.

Crime scene evidence went beyond mud. The Locard Principal states: "Every contact leaves a trace."[3] The goal of the forensic scientist is to link that trace evidence to its source, which may then lead to the suspect. This process is called individualization. The trace could be a cigarette, a hair, a thread, a footprint, even makeup, as was the case in one of Locard's most famous cases.

In 1912, Marie Latelle was found strangled to death in her parents' home. Police suspected her boyfriend, a bank clerk named Emile Gourbin. But the boyfriend had an alibi. He'd been playing cards with friends at a country home until after one a.m., and police knew that the murder had occurred before midnight. Locard examined the body and found scratches where the girl had been strangled—likely caused by fingernails. He visited Emile and scraped under his fingernails.

When Locard examined the scrapings under the microscope, he saw transparent flakes (skin cells) but also pink dust—makeup! Unlike today, when makeup is mass-produced by large cosmetic companies, Marie's face powder had been made locally by a druggist, so its ingredients were unique. Police took Marie's face powder to the lab. Chemical analysis showed that both the makeup and the fingernail scrapings contained rice starch, magnesium sterate, zinc oxide, bismuth, and Venetian red. The suspect confessed to murdering Marie. To secure an alibi from his fellow card players, he had moved the hands of the clock to show one a.m. when it was really only eleven thirty p.m. Emile claimed that he had visited Marie to ask her to marry him, and when she said no, he strangled her. But because he had moved back the clock, the murder was determined to be premeditated.

Another case in which trace evidence played a starring role was the murder of Germaine Bichon, a teenage girl living in Paris. One Sunday afternoon in July of 1909, a waiter at Café Bardin heard screaming in the apartment above. He told the café owner, Madame Bardin, but she waved it off as being nothing. Soon after, he felt something warm dripping on his head while washing dishes. When a drop fell on his arm, he saw that it was blood and exclaimed, "It's raining blood from Monsieur Albert's apartment!"[4]

The other café owner, Monsieur Bardin, called for the concierge, and together they ran upstairs to investigate. The door was locked, so the concierge summoned a police officer, and together they broke a window. Inside, they found Germaine beaten to death and lying in a pool of blood. A clean hatchet was found at the scene, which appeared to have been used to break into the victim's wardrobe. A money box had also been pried open. But there was no sign of the murderer having broken into the apartment.

On the desk was a letter:

> Dear sir, this letter is written by your little "Lolotte" who in a year has become your sweetheart. I want this letter to be a reminder to you of the year we have had together. You are thirty-four years old, I am seventeen. There have daily been more joys than sorrows. . . . These months have passed like a day. You have been like a father to me. I love you beyond reason. I feel as if I were your daughter.[5]

The rather disturbing love letter was addressed to the apartment owner, Albert Oursel. The age difference apparently wasn't criminal (though Germaine was in fact even younger—sixteen) but it certainly cast a suspicious light on Albert. Police learned that he ran an employment agency that placed maids in people's homes. Germaine had been one of those maids and had moved in with Albert, supposedly as his maid but actually as his girlfriend. She was head over heels for Albert, but the feelings weren't mutual, and he eventually broke up with her. Germaine had told friends that Albert wanted to get rid of her and was only letting her stay with him until he could find another job for her. Germaine was also pregnant.

Guilty as Albert may have seemed, the forensic evidence pointed to someone else. Germaine was found clutching several long blond and light brown hairs—likely a woman's. Hair evidence had been analyzed since the late 1850s, and by now, investigators could distinguish between human and animal hair and, in some cases, one person's hair from another's. Forensic scientists Victor Balthazard and Marcelle Lambert studied the hairs from the scene of the crime. In this case, all the hairs except one had a diameter ranging from .0024 to .0032 inches. One was unusually thick: .004 inches, and that was determined to belong to Germaine.

Seeking a female suspect, police met with Albert's real maid, Madame Dumouchet, who said that Albert had tired of Germaine but was too weak to kick her out. She suggested that police contact Albert's former maid Rosella, who had been a confidante to Germaine. Albert's secretary could put them in touch. As it turned out, Albert, Germaine, and the secretary were the only three people with keys to the apartment. The secretary worked until seven every evening, even on Saturdays, and the office was attached to Albert's apartment. That meant she was probably the last person to see Germaine alive. To complicate matters, Madame Dumouchet said the secretary didn't care for Germaine and was rumored to have a crush on Albert.

The secretary, Madame Dessignol, became a person of interest. The night before the murder, she had gone shopping with Germaine after work, and then Germaine had walked home alone. Dessignol said it was the last she saw of the teenage girl. Police asked if Germaine would have invited a stranger in that night. Dessignol said that while she didn't want to say anything bad about the dead, with Germaine, anything was possible. Police wrote in the margins "Hate? Jealousy?"[6] But any hopes of pinning the murder on the jealous secretary were dashed when Balthazard tested Dessignol's hairs—all were pale blond and too thin to be a match—.0024 inches or less.

Their attention, instead, turned to a mysterious woman named Angèle. The concierge said that soon after the murder was detected, the woman had stopped by the desk wearing a black scarf and asking after a servant who lived in the building. Angèle's hair was brownish blond—just like the hairs found on the body. The case was already sensational, but when the press picked up the story of Angèle, everyone was talking about the blond woman. However, they assumed she was an accomplice, as no one at the time could imagine a woman committing a violent murder on her own.

By now, Albert had returned. A balding man with a curly mustache, he copped to hiring Germaine as his maid with the intention of seducing her. He claimed that he hadn't realized she was only fifteen at the time. They had been together six months when he broke things off, telling her she needed to find new employment. He'd been letting her stay there temporarily, mostly ignoring her, which prompted her to write him love letters. He knew of the pregnancy but did not think the child was his. In spite of being a complete cad, it looked like he was innocent of the murder. He'd been visiting his mother in another town and had been seen out and about all day—having coffee, bicycling with a friend, and even spending the evening with the mayor. And anyway, there was the matter of the hair—definitely not Albert's. He showed police what had been stolen, including a gold ruble.

The police spoke to other maids in the neighborhood in hopes of finding the mysterious Angèle. The maids had a strange story: a woman named Madame Bosch had asked each of them to come with her to Albert's employment agency to collect wages owed to her. She wanted them to be witnesses when she confronted Albert. Her description matched that of Angèle. When the police finally tracked down Albert's former maid and Germaine's friend, Rosella Rousseau, they learned that her previous name (by marriage) was Madame Bosch. Could she be Angèle, too?

Neither the maids nor the concierge could say whether Rousseau was the mysterious Madame Bosch or Angèle. Police questioned Rousseau nonetheless, and she gave a rather unflattering alibi. She had gone to an uncle's to borrow money, and when he refused, she stole it from him. The uncle was too senile to confirm the visit. Rousseau sobbed when police brought up the murder, saying that she loved Germaine like a daughter.

A neighborhood café owner finally cracked open the hard nut that was Rousseau. He said that Rousseau owed all the cafés money and that her landlord had given her an ultimatum: pay up or get out.

She'd turned up at the café on Sunday, paying part of her debt and drinking several glasses of wine. Then she went to sell something to a peddler. The peddler told police that Rousseau had tried to sell him a coin, but he didn't purchase it. Could it have been the stolen gold ruble?

Balthazard tested Rousseau's hair. It was a match—blond and brown in front and the right thickness. At first Rousseau didn't admit to the crime. But when the detective held up the hairs, she broke down. She said she'd sneaked into Albert's office the day before. She watched Germaine and the secretary leave but didn't steal anything because she was worried that Germaine would soon return. When Germaine finally did come back, she locked the door between the office and living space. Rousseau was now trapped in the office and would have to wait until morning to get to the wardrobe in the bedroom, where she was sure the money was hidden.

The next day, when Germaine opened the door between the office and the apartment, Rousseau sneaked into the dining room. She hoped to evade Germaine, but the teenager was sitting there, eating a sausage. Rousseau lunged for Germaine, who picked up the hatchet in self-defense. Rousseau grabbed it and beat the girl with it. Rousseau then stole what she could find, washed her clothes and the hatchet, and sneaked out amid the hubbub of the murder investigation, leaving a fake name with the concierge so that she would have a reason for being in the building. She was found guilty and sentenced to death.

Random hairs are commonly found at crime scenes, not surprisingly, as hair can be pulled out during a struggle, or fall out undetected (people lose an average of a hundred hairs a day).

Nowadays, hairs can be analyzed for their chemical makeup through DNA testing. Prior to that becoming available, scientists could only compare hairs based on their physical characteristics. In addition to thickness, experts could observe whether a hair was cut with scissors or a razor, and whether it was dyed (and how long ago based on the length of undyed hair toward the root). Even with such a detailed analysis, hair couldn't be linked to any one person. That's because two people's hair can be very similar. But hair analysis could be used to rule out—or rule in—suspects. In the French case, it indeed ruled out the secretary and led to Rousseau's confession.

Perhaps surprisingly, a thread from a rug, a rope, or fabric could be just as helpful in solving a crime—if not more so—than a hair in the days before DNA testing. Whereas all hairs are made of the protein keratin, fibers can be made from a variety of materials. Wool, hemp, cotton, polyester, and nylon are just a handful of options. The color of the thread can also indicate whether a unique pattern or dye was used. Once the makeup of the fiber is determined, investigators can link it to a manufacturer, who can then provide a record of sales that may lead to a buyer—and a suspect. Today, a thread may lead to a manufacturer that sells the fabric so widely that anyone could have bought it. But historically, manufacturers were smaller and sold their products regionally. Let's look at how both a hair and a thread helped unravel a 1930s murder mystery in New York.

Things were happening for Nancy Titterton. She was happily married to an NBC radio executive, with whom she shared a love of reading and writing. After having a short story published in *Story* magazine, Nancy had just been awarded her first book contract. She would never see the book released. On April 10, 1936, Nancy was found strangled to death in her apartment. She is thought to have been writing the book at the time of death—a fountain pen was found on her pillow. Sixty-five detectives were assigned to the case, but it was the New York Medical Examiner's Office that cracked it open.

Nancy Titterton, whose strangled body was found in the bathtub of her New York City apartment

Detectives determined that Nancy had been attacked in the bedroom and dragged to the bathroom. Two key pieces of evidence were found. A thirteen-inch cord lay beneath the body, and a light-colored hair was on the bedspread. Detectives assumed the hair was Nancy's, but looking at it under the microscope, assistant medical examiner Dr. Benjamin Morgan Vance saw that it was too coarse to be human. Rather, it was horsehair. At the time, horsehair was used to stuff furniture.

That was an important clue. Nancy's body had been found by two men delivering a couch: upholsterer Theodore Kruger and his assistant, Johnny Fiorenza. They'd also been to the apartment the day before to pick up the old couch. But they hadn't entered the bedroom, which was at the opposite end of the apartment. Investigators wondered if the cord could be linked to the upholsterers in a more nefarious way. It was one-eighth of an inch wide and woven from Italian hemp and jute. Police sent a note to twenty-five rope makers in the New York City region. A week later, Hanover Cordage

Company of York, Pennsylvania, told police that their company made that type of rope and sold it to several upholsterers. Police took a sample to Hanover Cordage. It matched the rope there. The company had a record of selling the cord to a wholesaler in New York, who in turn had sold it to Theodore Kruger, the upholsterer who'd delivered the sofa.

Soon, the police homed in on Theodore's assistant Johnny, a painfully shy young man who had dropped out of grade school and spent time in prison for theft. Though the crime wasn't violent, a prison psychiatrist called Johnny a "potential psychotic" who could turn violent one day.

Love seat that was used as evidence against Johnny Fiorenza for the murder of Nancy Titterton

He now lived with his mother in the Bensonhurst neighborhood of Brooklyn and, according to Theodore, was a reliable and trustworthy worker.

Sadly, the psychiatrist's prediction had come true. Ten days after the murder, Johnny confessed. When he had first seen Nancy in her apartment, he'd had evil thoughts. The next day, he returned at ten thirty in the morning, pretending to be there to take more measurements. When Nancy let him in, he assaulted and killed her. Five hours later, he accompanied his boss to deliver the couch. He had hoped that by finding the body, he would escape suspicion. But he had unwittingly left that thread of evidence.

Johnny Fiorenza (center) leaving New York City for Sing Sing Prison

Decades later, in 1981, fibers would lead to the arrest of an elusive serial killer. Police were investigating a string of murders of young men and boys. The method of murder differed in each case, but they were all linked by threads found on the bodies. Some were yellow-green and nylon, and others violet and acetate. Investigators talked to textile experts about where such threads might have come from. The killer must have read media reports of the textile investigation, because he began dumping his victims in the river, apparently so that the threads would wash away. The police began staking out bridges, and one night, an officer heard a splash. He arrested the only man driving across the bridge at the time: Wayne Williams. Williams said that he'd dumped garbage, but two days later, a body was found.

Police got a search warrant, and in Williams's home they found what turned out to be a limited edition yellow-green carpet. Odds were one in 7,792 that it would be found by random selection. In addition, the violet threads matched Williams's bedspread. In all, twenty-eight fibers linked Williams to the murders, including hair from his German shepherd. It became more and more likely that Williams was the killer.

The body of one of Wayne Williams's victims
is pulled from the Chattahoochee River.

In forensic science, there is a product rule. It considers the chances that each piece of evidence would occur randomly and then multiplies those chances. Let's say that a red Ford truck was seen fleeing the scene of a bank robbery. Hypothetically, if one in ten vehicles on the road is a Ford, and one in eighteen is red, and one in twelve is a truck, then by multiplying 10, 18, and 12, there is a one in 2,160 chance that a red Ford truck found by police officers is the same truck seen fleeing the scene. The fact that so many fibers were found on the bodies of the murder victims, and in Williams's home, increased the odds that he was the murderer, and indeed, he was convicted, though he has maintained his innocence.

Another type of crime scene evidence involves impressions. These include shoe prints, tire prints, weapon marks, bite marks, and more. In forensic science, there is a maxim that no two objects—whether natural or manmade—are alike, and so they don't leave the same mark. According to this theory, even two tires manufactured side by side in the same factory will leave slightly different tread marks on a muddy road. Legal experts are now questioning whether this theory is true in practice. While two items may leave different marks, the marks may be so similar as to be indistinguishable by an expert. Such expert testimony has been proven to be faulty by DNA evidence. But such marks can at least narrow down the pool of suspects to, say, those who wear a certain brand of shoe.

That was the case in the brutal murder of gas station worker Liaquat Ali in 1992. Rockland County medical examiner Frederick Zugibe was called to the scene after a driver found the victim dead at the gas station and called police. Ali's injuries revealed that he had been beaten with a broomstick and garbage can lid, stabbed with a broomstick and a knife, and doused with industrial fluid, which burned his eyes and face. It had been an unthinkably violent attack, and Zugibe wondered if there were other injuries as well. He searched the body using different kinds of light, including ultraviolet. This would reveal semen, saliva, and blood, along with handprints, footprints, and shoe prints. In this case, he found the impression of a shoe tread spelling N-I-K. One suspect, Raymond Navarro, owned a pair of Nikes. They were brought to the lab and tested for blood cells. Blood cells are nearly impossible to wash away, and sure enough, blood was in the treads of Navarro's shoe. A DNA test revealed it to be Ali's. Police learned that Navarro, along with his pal Michael Moore, had tried to rob the gas station cash register, and when Ali fought back, they threw industrial fluid in his face, beat him, and stabbed him. After this senseless attack, Navarro and Moore pocketed just fifty dollars, a roll of quarters, four packs of cigarettes, and two lighters.

5

Fingerprints Are Forever: Early Fingerprint Evidence

Of the many types of evidence at a crime scene, one of the most personal is the fingerprint. Or at least, that was true before DNA testing. Fingerprints remain the same throughout a person's life. To avoid being identified, criminals have tried obliterating their fingerprints. But even mutilated fingerprints can be used to identify a suspect. John Dillinger, a bank robber, escaped convict, and cop killer, succeeded somewhat in burning his fingerprints off with acid, but this only made them more unique to him because of the scarring. And when Dillinger was shot and killed by FBI agents, his fingerprint patterns could still be seen around the edges of his fingertips. To this day, some criminals still have skin grafted onto their fingertips. Though this eliminates the need to wear gloves to a crime scene, it's hardly helpful during an arrest. The absence of fingerprints is fishy to say the least.

Before fingerprints were discovered, the police had a hard time keeping track of known criminals. They needed a way of identifying repeat offenders so that they could receive harsher sentences. A name wasn't enough. The criminal could give a fake one. At first, police turned to photography, a process invented in the 1820s and 30s. But there were limits to that. Two people could look an awful lot alike, and a person's appearance could change over time, or be altered by growing a beard, for instance.

Eventually, a forensic scientist for the Sûreté, Alphonse Bertillon, developed a more precise method. Bertillon came from a family of scientists, and his grandfather often said that no two humans have the same physical measurements. Working on that belief, Bertillon created an identification system that was unique to each criminal. It involved measuring the convict's height, left arm from the elbow to the tip of the middle finger, head circumference, ear length, and more. With so many measurements, the odds were one in 286 million that any two people would have the same measurements. In its

first year, his system, called Bertillonage, identified three hundred repeat offenders the police would have otherwise missed. The method spread to crime bureaus throughout the world.

At the same time, a new method of identification was slowly taking shape. People in ancient China and Japan understood that fingerprints were unique to each person. In China, important documents were sealed with clay, upon

Bertillon measurement being taken

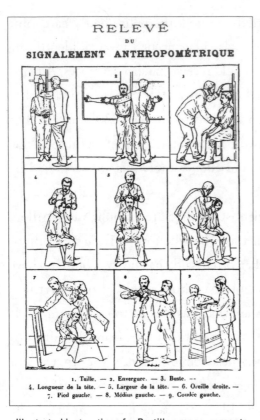

RELEVÉ
DU
SIGNALEMENT ANTHROPOMÉTRIQUE

1. Taille. — 2. Envergure. — 3. Buste. —
4. Longueur de la tête. — 5. Largeur de la tête. — 6. Oreille droite. —
7. Pied gauche. — 8. Médius gauche. — 9. Coudée gauche.

Illustrated instructions for Bertillon measurements

which the author impressed a fingerprint to show authenticity. As early as 221 BCE a crime scene handbook told how handprints could be used to solve a crime. The importance of finger-prints came to be known much later in the West. Much has been made about who was the father of fingerprints in the West. That's because several people working independently of each other made discoveries in this area.

William Herschel was an Englishman working in India in the mid-1800s when he began collecting and studying the finger-prints of family, friends, and colleagues. When he was appointed to a government position, he used fingerprints to identify people in the criminal courts, prisons, and pension office. He would go on to study fingerprints throughout his life and was able to show that a person's fingerprints remained constant over time. In America, scien-tist Thomas Taylor gave a lecture on how fingerprints found at crime scenes could be matched to suspects. It was published in an 1877 issue of the *American Journal of Microscopy and Popular Science*.

Around the same time, Dr. Henry Faulds, a Scotsman working as a missionary doctor in Japan, became interested in fingerprints when he saw that Japanese potters used fingerprints as signatures on their work. In 1880, he wrote a letter to the journal *Nature* describing "the skin-furrows of the hand" and telling how to take fingerprints and how they might be used to identify criminals.[1] In fact, he wrote that he himself had used fingerprints to discover a thief in his own hospital. Someone had stolen surgical alcohol from a bottle and left their greasy fingerprints behind. He was able to match the prints on the bottle to an employee. Despite Faulds's advances, Herschel would become a bigger name in the burgeoning field of fingerprints, a fact that would infuriate Faulds for many years.

In the 1880s, prominent British scientist—and cousin to Charles Darwin—Sir Francis Galton, contacted Herschel about collaborating on a study of fingerprints. Galton, too, had been collecting fingerprints, and together they had the largest collection in the world. Galton studied whether fingerprints really were unchanging, unique to individuals, and classifiable, so that they could be matched to their owners. Through his research, he found the answer to all these questions to be yes, and he reported this in many books and articles.

After reading Galton's work, Argentinian police official Juan Vucetich began fingerprinting prisoners and filing the prints under his own classification system—the first of its kind in the world. He was also the first to solve a murder in modern times using fingerprints. In 1892, two children were found murdered in the coastal town of Necochea. Their mother, Francesca Rojas, had a throat wound. When questioned, she accused a man named Velasquez of attacking the children and her. But even during a brutal interrogation that included being tied to the corpses over-night, Velasquez maintained his innocence. Officer Eduardo Alvarez inspected the crime scene and found a bloody thumbprint on the door. He called in Vucetich, who matched the fingerprint to Francesca. Upon seeing the evidence, she confessed to killing her own children.

Elsewhere, fingerprints didn't replace Bertillonage right away as a method for identifying criminals. In America, the shift was made after the case of the two Will Wests. In 1903, a man named Will West was admitted to Leavenworth Penitentiary. His Bertillon measurements were taken, and they matched those of a man already in prison, *William* West. Had he escaped? Nope, he was safe in bed. Now the prison had a case of two men with matching Bertillon measurements. The men claimed they were not related, though they looked alike and had the same name. Their fingerprints, on the other hand, were different. Because of this, fingerprint advocates said that a switch to the fingerprint system was needed. Fingerprinting overtook

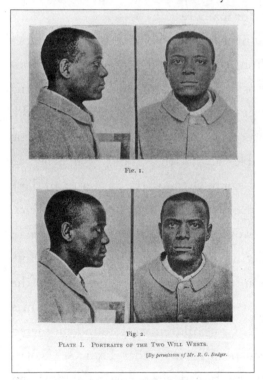

Fig. 1.

Fig. 2.

PLATE I. PORTRAITS OF THE TWO WILL WESTS.

[By permission of Mr. R. G. Badger.

Portraits of the two Will Wests

Bertillonage the following year, and a fingerprint registry of all federal prison inmates was established in Leavenworth.

With the odds being one in 286 million that two people would have the same Bertillon measurements, and the world population at the time being about 1.6 billion, it was possible for two people to coincidentally match up. In this case, the "coincidence" was more like the joke about the Irish brothers. They're in a bar, comparing the remarkable similarities in their lives—they went to the same school! They graduated the same year! They even grew up on the same street! And in the same house! Then the bartender remarks that the O'Malley twins are drunk again. It turns out the two Will Wests had twin Bertillon measurements because they *were* twins. A fellow prisoner testified that they were; and correspondence logs showed that the two men wrote to the same brother, five sisters, and an Uncle George. This problem probably wouldn't have come up much, as identical twins, and certainly identical twin criminals, are rare. And so whether this case actually was the impetus for the switch from Bertillonage to fingerprinting is debatable. The fact is, Bertillonage's drawbacks were becoming all too clear. It was time-consuming. And people didn't leave their measurements at crime scenes. They *did* leave their fingerprints.

By 1894, all criminals in England and Bengal (then under British domain) were fingerprinted. Bengali police inspector Sir Edward Richard Henry worked with Galton to classify the fingerprints of criminals, and it was here that fingerprint evidence was first used to convict a criminal in court. The manager of a tea garden was found in bed with his throat cut, the victim of a robbery. The suspects were a veritable cast of Clue characters. It could have been any of the garden employees, for the man was said to be a mean boss; an ex-employee who had recently been released from jail; the cook, who had bloodstains on his clothes; the relatives of a woman with whom the man was having an affair; or a gang of criminals that had been hanging around the neighborhood.

The cook explained that it was pigeon blood on his clothing— dinner that night. By now, there was a blood test to differentiate between human and animal blood, and it proved that the cook was telling the truth. Likewise, the woman's relatives and the gang of criminals were cleared. Police turned their attention to the ex-employee/ex-convict. They found a calendar among the man's items that had been rifled through, and on it, human blood and finger-prints. The fingerprints matched those of the ex-employee, Kangali Charan. Charan was convicted of theft, but not murder, as the judge ruled that only the first had been proven.

In England, fingerprint evidence was first used to solve a murder in 1905. An elderly couple, Thomas and Ann Farrow, lived above their paint shop in Deptford, just outside of London. On March 27, 1905, one of their workers arrived to find Thomas lying in the shop and Ann, upstairs in the apartment, both beaten and bloody. Thomas was dead. Ann was unconscious and would die four days later without regaining consciousness. Could forensic science tell the couple's tragic story?

The motive was clear: robbery. The shop's cashbox had been emptied. Scotland Yard found on the box a thumbprint, matching neither the victims' nor any fingerprints on file. Police pounded the pavement in search of witnesses. A milkman said he'd seen two young men leaving the shop the day of the murder. He'd told them they'd left the door open, but the men said there was another person coming behind them. Another eyewitness, Ellen Stanton, said she'd seen two men running at around the time of the murders. She knew one of them to be Alfred Stratton. He and his brother Albert were now suspects. The milkman was unable to identify them, but Albert's thumbprint matched the one found at the scene.

Interestingly, Henry Faulds—the man who had written *Nature* about his discovery of fingerprints—testified for the defense. He said that a single smudged print left behind at a crime scene was difficult to match to a complete print. He did not think that such evidence was reliable enough to convict someone of murder (a matter that is still being debated today). The judge himself said that the men shouldn't be found guilty based on the fingerprint alone, and yet guilty the verdict was.

Jurors came to accept fingerprint evidence more and more. In America, the effectiveness of fingerprint analysis was proven in dramatic fashion during the 1911 burglary trial of Charles Crispi. Expert witness Joseph Faurot said that a fingerprint left on a glass door at the crime scene belonged to Charles. Fingerprint evidence was new, so Faurot wanted to show jurors that he knew his stuff. He took the jurors' fingerprints and then left the room while they pressed their fingers onto glass. When Faurot came back into the courtroom, he was able to match each print on the glass to the correct juror. He then walked the jury through his methods of fingerprint matching. After the demonstration, Crispi changed his plea to guilty.

As news of fingerprint evidence spread, criminals became savvier, wearing gloves or wiping down surfaces they touched. But nobody is perfect. In 1963, fifteen men robbed a British mail train, in an

Ocean's 11–style heist known as the Great Train Robbery. They made away with £2.6 million in cash ($4 million then, about $31 million today). Afterward, they hid out in a farmhouse, passing the time playing Monopoly with real money. By the time police arrived, the

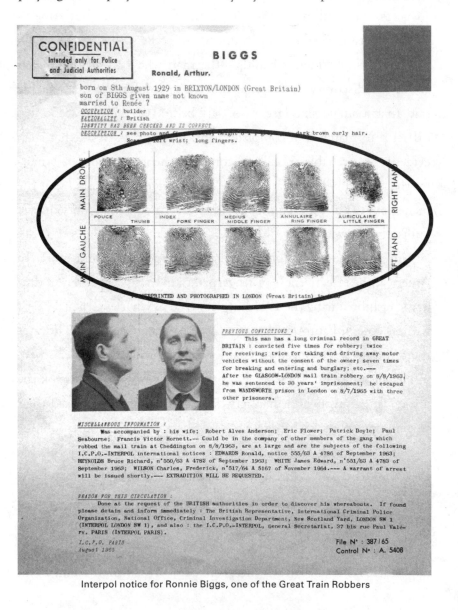

Interpol notice for Ronnie Biggs, one of the Great Train Robbers

men had gotten away—and they'd had the good sense to wipe off any fingerprints. Or so they thought. Police found fingerprints on the Monopoly board, which led to the arrest of the fifteen, although two later escaped from prison.

In one case, a criminal needed to conceal not his own fingerprints but those of another man. Charles Henry Schwartz was a California inventor who seemed to be doing well. He owned his own company—one of the first to create a formula for artificial silk. Then, on July 30, 1925, his lab exploded with him in it. Or so it seemed. The inventor's wife identified the body as belonging to her husband. And famous crime scene investigator Edward Oscar Heinrich matched the corpse's missing teeth to Charles's dental records.

Then Heinrich made some strange discoveries: the victim had been killed with a blunt instrument prior to being burned. In addition, the eyes had been gouged out and the fingerprints doused in acid. At the scene, police found a Bible belonging to Gilbert Barbe, a traveling missionary. They now believed the dead body to be Gilbert's and not Charles's. Heinrich sought a photo of Charles from his wife. She gave him the only

Police stand guard outside a hideout used by the Great Train Robbers

one she could find (the rest had disappeared). When the photo ran in the newspaper, Charles's luck ran out.

Charles had been living a double life as Harold Warren, a ladies' man and party guy. Under that name, he'd befriended the Haywards, who owned a boardinghouse. Recently, he'd come to them saying he'd been in an accident and couldn't call police because there was liquor in his car (this was during Prohibition). He needed a place to rest and recuperate. "Harold" must not have been feeling too badly, however, because he was the life of the party while at the Haywards'.

Mr. Hayward later described how Harold had behaved at a surprise party for the Haywards' daughter: "He joked, laughed and mixed freely with the guests. He mixed punch, invented new games, and even led the 'grand march,' stalking along gaily at the head of the group."[2]

But the party would soon be over for Fun Harold. At a dinner party with other friends, Mr. Hayward mentioned that one of his lodgers was hiding out after being in an accident that involved whiskey. The subject of Charles Schwartz, who was also hiding out, as reported by all the newspapers, came up. Mr. Hayward said he had no idea what the wanted man looked like, and someone showed him the picture. It was Harold! Mr. Hayward alerted police that Charles Schwartz was staying at the boardinghouse.

Police surrounded the house, but before they could arrest Charles, he shot himself. In his pocket was a letter to his wife. He claimed that he'd killed Gilbert Barbe in self-defense, after the traveling preacher demanded money. He explained that he had come home afterward and taken his photos and other belongings. "Now I wish to tell you, my dear little girl. I do not know the man, never looked how he was dressed, never touched him after that. The only thing I did was, I tried to burn him, to wipe him out and go—go, I do not know where."[3]

But he hadn't "only" burned the body. He'd also poured acid on the fingertips, gouged out the eyes, and pulled one of the teeth, and then gone home for the family photos, all extremely odd things to do after killing someone in self-defense. Schwartz had really faked his own death to collect his life insurance, which included double-indemnity clauses, meaning an accident would double the payout of the claim. In all, the policies totaled more than $100,000, which would have come in handy, because, as it turned out, the artificial silk business wasn't going so hot. Though Charles obliterated Gilbert's identifying features, he failed to do much about his own appearance (other than grow a mustache). And that's what got him in the end.

In 1924, the fingerprints from Leavenworth and other US law agencies were combined under the newly formed Identification Division of the US Bureau of Investigation. J. Edgar Hoover led this division and would go on to become the longtime director of the bureau, which was renamed the FBI in 1935. It's common for a convict to break the law again, and if that happened, the FBI would be able to link a fingerprint found at the crime scene to the past offender. During Hoover's tenure, the FBI's Fingerprint Bureau collected 200 million prints. In those days, detectives had to search for fingerprints through an elaborate filing system. Now, the FBI and other law enforcement agencies can search by computer—usually. A fingerprint led to the arrest of serial killer Aileen Wuornos in 1990—but investigators had to search for the match the old-fashioned way.

Aileen wasn't the first female serial killer. But she was unique in that her victims were strangers and her weapon of choice was a gun. Blaming psychopathic behavior on a bad childhood may be cliché, but in Aileen's case, it fits the bill. Aileen's mother abandoned her, and her father, a convicted child molester, hanged himself in prison. Aileen went to live with her grandparents. She said that while in their care, she was abused by her grandfather. She became pregnant at age thirteen—the result of rape—and the baby was placed for adoption. By age sixteen, she was supporting herself as a highway prostitute and showing signs of psychosis. Her tragic childhood gave way to an aggressive adulthood. By the time she was investigated for murder, her record included armed robbery, grand theft auto, resisting arrest, assault and battery, and firing a pistol from a moving car. Her crimes would only get worse.

Aileen Wuornos, who was executed by lethal injection for murdering six men

On December 13, 1989, two men scavenging for scrap metal spotted a buzzard and smelled something rotten. As one of the men said in a note for investigators: "Trompeding [tromping] through the woods we smelled stink! I was off troming [roaming?] through the Palms when my friend yelled for me and sed look! I saw a tarp [tarpaulin] with a hand hanging out of It!"[4]

They had discovered the body of Richard Mallory, dead from a gunshot wound. Within the next year, six other gunshot victims would be found—all men. The killer didn't go entirely undetected. On July 4, witnesses saw two women leaving the car of the fourth victim. They gave a description to a police artist, and Florida detectives released the sketch to the press. The women were identified by callers as Lee Blahovec and Tyria Moore.

At around the same time, a sheriff's officer was checking pawn shops for the victims' belongings. He found a camera and radar detector that had belonged to the first victim, Richard Mallory. As required by law, the seller had left her right thumbprint on the receipt, along with her name, Cammie Marsh Greene. Unfortunately, Florida investigators couldn't find a match in the computer system. Fingerprint expert Jennie Ahern, of the Florida Department of Law Enforcement's Orlando Regional Crime Laboratory, and colleagues Debbie Fischer and David Perry had to search for fingerprints the old-fashioned way.

They visited local law enforcement agencies and flipped through cards on file. As luck would have it, they found a match at the first place they looked: the Volusia County Sheriff's Office. The name on the card said Lori Kristine Grody. The experts searched jail records for a photo. It turned out Lori, Lee, and Cammie were one and the same. And none would turn out to be the woman's real name. When the experts ran Lori's record through the FBI's National Crime Information Center, they found a match for Aileen Carol Wuornos, whose record began when she was still a juvenile. Police found Aileen at the aptly named bar the Last Resort and arrested her. She confessed to the killings in hopes that her friend Tyria wouldn't stand accused. Aileen insisted that she killed the men in self-defense, but the jury didn't believe it. Aileen was put to death in 2002.

As helpful as fingerprints can be, they can also lead investigators astray. It's one thing to match a full thumbprint—intentionally left on a pawn shop receipt—to a fingerprint on file. But partial prints are difficult to match. The same questions raised in the Stratton brothers' case are still being raised today. Is fingerprint evidence reliable enough to convict someone of murder? After all, fingerprints have sometimes led to the wrong suspect.

Exterior shot of the Last Resort bar, where Aileen Wuornos was arrested

One such case involved a terrorist investigation. On March 11, 2004, four commuter trains were bombed in Madrid, killing 191 people and injuring more than 1,800. Spanish investigators arrested several suspects. They also shared fingerprints found at the scene with the FBI. The FBI ran the prints and got twenty potential matches, including Oregon attorney Brandon Mayfield, whose fingerprints were on file because he had served in the US Army. In a side-by-side comparison, Mayfield's fingerprint was believed to match one of the fingerprints found at the scene.

The FBI ordered 24-hour surveillance on Mayfield. They learned that he was a Muslim married to an Egyptian immigrant and that he had represented a convicted terrorist in a child custody case. These factors would color the investigation moving forward. Though

Spanish fingerprint experts did not think Mayfield's fingerprint was a match, and no other evidence linked him to the attack, the FBI pressed on in their investigation. When reporters began inquiring about a possible American suspect, the FBI feared Mayfield would flee. They detained him as a material witness and then arrested him on May 6. Then on May 19, Spanish investigators matched the fingerprint to Algerian national Ouhnane Daoud. A court released Mayfield to home detention, and on May 24, the FBI dismissed all proceedings against him.

Rescue workers search through the wreckage of
a bombed commuter train in Madrid, Spain.

In October of 2004, Mayfield filed a civil action against the FBI, the Department of Justice, and several individuals for violations of his civil rights, the Privacy Act, and his constitutional rights. How could investigators have been so wrong about the fingerprints? An internal investigation by the US Department of Justice said that the

FBI fingerprint analysts focused too much on similarities and not enough on differences between the two prints. They tried to explain away the differences, saying, for instance, that the fingerprint must have been overlaid by another person's fingerprint, even though the evidence showed they were looking at a single print. The report also said that the FBI should have gone back to the drawing board when the Spanish National Police said that the two fingerprints didn't match. But their judgment was clouded by what they had learned about Mayfield's personal life.

Though fingerprint evidence has been used for more than a hundred years, this case shows that mistakes can still be made. Forensic evidence isn't perfect. Comparing fingerprints requires judgment on the part of the expert, and history shows that bias can cloud that judgment. Since the Mayfield case, fingerprint technology has improved. According to the FBI, its new system for finding fingerprint matches, Next Generation Identification, has a better computer algorithm for generating matches. As such, it has reduced the number of instances that require manual fingerprint reviews by several percentage points. The system also includes 23 million mug shots and, in the future, will allow for identification through iris recognition.

Fingerprinting was well underway at the FBI when another forensic science tool came into play: firearm analysis.

Bang! Bang! You're Dead: The Birth of Firearm Analysis

If poison deaths were rampant at the turn of the twentieth century, gun deaths are now. Every day in America, an average of 31 people are murdered with a gun, and 151 wounded by intentional gunfire. Many more are victims of suicide and accidental shootings. Needless to say, firearm analysis is an important component of forensic science.

Investigators first used firearm evidence to solve a murder case in 1794. A surgeon in Lancashire, England, was performing an autopsy on a gunshot wound victim when he found paper in the wound. At the time, guns fired one shot only. To load the gun, you would pour the gunpowder into the barrel, drop in a round bullet, add a wad of paper to hold everything in place, and then tamp it all down with a ramrod. In this case, the piece of paper had been torn from a street ballad, and the suspect had the other piece of the ballad in his pocket.

Round bullets

He was arrested. Such wads of paper surely could have been traced to suspects in other cases. Unfortunately, new guns were invented that didn't require paper. Then, in 1888, investigators learned that the bullets themselves were important clues. Alexandre Lacassagne (a familiar name by now) was performing an autopsy of seventy-eight-year-old Claude Moiroud and found three bullets—one in the larynx, one in the shoulder, and another near the spine. He noticed that each had the same grooves. The bullet markings couldn't have been caused by the body, since each bullet went through a different part. Could the gun have caused the markings? Lacassagne contacted a gun maker, who explained that guns were designed to have spiral grooves in the barrels. These grooves, known as rifling, made the bullets spin, resulting in more accurate shots. The rifling also left indentations on the bullets. It was a light-bulb moment for Lacassagne. It meant bullets could be linked to their corresponding guns.

In the meantime, police had received a tip about the Moiroud case: a woman was hiding a gun for her boyfriend in her home. Officers seized the gun, which belonged to a man named Echallier, and gave it to Lacassagne for

Rifling in a machine gun barrel

testing. Lacassagne fired bullets into a cadaver and found that the bullets had the same grooves as those found in Moiroud. Based on this evidence, Echallier was convicted. Lacassagne also asked a student to research the markings found on fired bullets. Together, the two men published a scientific article on the subject, which matched twenty-six bullets to their respective guns.

As usual, France was ahead of the game. In America, the science of firearm analysis lagged behind. The implications of this became clear when an innocent man was sentenced to death for murder. On March 22, 1915, a farmhand, Charlie Stielow, found his elderly employer, Charles Phelps, and the man's housekeeper, Margaret Wallcott, shot to death. Police determined the weapon to be a .22-caliber revolver. Charlie said that he didn't own a gun, which police soon discovered to be a lie. Charlie was arrested. Police called in firearms expert Dr. Albert Hamilton, though both "Dr." and "expert" were a bit of a stretch. Hamilton called himself a doctor but hadn't even graduated from high school. He advertised himself as an expert in firearms and more, though he had neither training nor experience in any of these fields. Hamilton "examined" the gun and bullets and declared them to be a match.

During interrogation, the farmhand confessed. The cards were stacked against him, though. For one thing, he was a native of Germany and spoke little English. He was also considered to be learning disabled (though that assumption may have been due to the language barrier). At trial, his attorney argued that the confession was coerced, but the judge allowed it into evidence. To make matters worse, Hamilton testified that Charlie's revolver had definitely fired the bullets. He said that he had found nine bumps in the barrel of

Charlie's revolver and nine corresponding indentations on the bullets taken from the shooting victims. He explained that the jury would be unable to see these scratches with their own eyes. "I can tell because I am a highly technical man," he said. "I can see what the jury cannot see."[1]

Charlie was found guilty and sentenced to death. But while he awaited execution, several good Samaritans investigated his cause. They learned that two tramps, Erwin King and Clarence O'Connell, had been in the area at the time of the murders. The tramps confessed to police but later retracted their confessions. Nevertheless, New York governor Charles Whitman granted a stay of execution so that the case could be reexamined. Charles Waite, who worked for the New York attorney general, was brought in to reexamine the firearm evidence.

Waite took the gun and bullets to New York City police firearms expert Henry Jones, who immediately saw the problem. Charlie's gun hadn't been fired in years. Nevertheless, Jones fired the gun and examined the bullets. They looked nothing like the bullets found in the body. Based on this evidence, the governor ordered Charlie to be released from prison.

Though the story had a happy ending, Waite was struck by the fact that an innocent man was imprisoned and nearly put to death due to unscientific firearm analysis. Inspired to change the system, he cataloged all American handguns, and then the European models sold in America. To examine the insides of gun barrels, he used a newly invented helixometer, a tube with a magnifier on the end. Waite, along with Calvin Goddard and other colleagues, established the Bureau of Forensic Ballistics in New York in 1923.

Waite died just three years later, but Goddard went on to analyze firearms in several major cases, including the trial of Sacco and Vanzetti, two anarchists accused of robbery and murder. April 15, 1920, was payday at the Slater & Morrill shoe factory. Around three p.m., paymaster Frederick Parmenter and armed guard Alexander Berardelli were carrying two boxes containing wages totaling $15,776.51 from the company's office to its factory in South Braintree, Massachusetts. Two men shot and killed Parmenter and Berardelli, and as they did, a getaway car pulled up with several men inside. The two gunmen loaded the boxes into the car, jumped in, and sped away. The getaway car was found two days later in the woods.

Police at the time were investigating a similar robbery in nearby Bridgewater. In that case, the getaway car—a Buick—had sped off toward Cochesett. In both cases, witnesses said the gang members were Italian. So police were looking for an Italian owning a Buick in Cochesett. This led them to Mario Boda, an anarchist, and his friends Nicola Sacco, twenty-nine, and Bartolomeo Vanzetti, thirty-two, also anarchists.

In the late 1910s and early 1920s, anarchists were a formidable group. They believed that the capitalist system oppressed laborers and needed to be overthrown, and that the war in Europe was immoral. Americans feared that anarchists would attempt a revolution similar to the Bolshevik Revolution in Russia, which led to the deadliest civil war in history and the brutal assassination of the royal Romanov family. In America, during a period known as the Red Scare, several anarchists were arrested, detained, and deported based on their beliefs alone. To protest these arrests, anarchist groups planned attacks against government officials and wealthy businessmen like John D. Rockefeller. For instance, anarchist Carlo Valdinoci, a friend of Boda, Sacco, and Vanzetti, blew himself up in a suicide bombing of Attorney General A. Mitchell Palmer's home on June 2, 1919.

That bombing only escalated the arrests, and another friend of the three anarchists, Andrea Salsedo, was detained by the US Department of Justice for several weeks and beaten until he gave information. He jumped from the Justice Department building (or possibly was pushed) to his death on May 3, 1920. Worried that Salsedo might have shared incriminating evidence against them, the three planned to hide their anarchist literature—and possibly the supplies for a planned attack—and warn others to do the same. To carry this out, they headed to the garage to pick up Boda's car. A garage worker informed the police, and the police then tracked down Sacco and Vanzetti, and a third man, Riccardo Orciani. Boda escaped.

Sacco, Vanzetti, and Orciani were now held as suspects in both robberies. Orciani had an alibi and was released. Sacco, who worked at another shoe factory, had worked the day of the first robbery, but taken the day off on April 15. Vanzetti, a fishmonger, said he had been working, but the police didn't believe him, and so he would be tried for the Bridgewater robbery. Both Sacco and Vanzetti were indicted for the Braintree robbery. To protest, Boda set off a bomb in a horse and buggy in Manhattan, killing thirty people and injuring many more.

The trial began May 31, 1921. It would last seven weeks and make news worldwide. Some believed that Sacco and Vanzetti's arrest and prosecution had nothing to do with the robbery, but was punishment for their anarchist activities. Indeed, their political beliefs were targeted by the prosecutors, who questioned the defendants about dodging the draft (both Sacco and Vanzetti had fled to Mexico to avoid going to war) and owning anarchist literature. Even the judge seemed set against the defendants. At one point, he was heard saying outside the courtroom, "Did you see what I did with those anarchistic bastards the other day? I guess that will hold them for a while."[2]

Italian anarchists Nicola Sacco and Bartolomeo Vanzetti
behind prison bars before their executions

The trial itself was a battle of the eyewitnesses. Fifty-nine people testified for the prosecution and ninety-nine for the defense. They told very different stories. For instance, six witnesses said they saw Vanzetti selling fish in Plymouth on April 15 at the time of the

Protestors showing support for Sacco and Vanzetti after their conviction

crime, but another four said they saw him near the scene of the crime. Felix Frankfurter, a Harvard law professor who would go on to become a US Supreme Court justice, was a vocal supporter of Sacco and Vanzetti. He explained that the reliance on eyewitnesses in the case was unwise. Eyewitness identification of strangers, particularly those of a "foreign race" (referring to the fact that Sacco and Vanzetti were Italian), is notoriously unreliable, he said. Case in point: One of the prosecutor's star eyewitnesses, Lola Andrews, identified Sacco as being near the scene of the crime at the time of the shooting. But a shopkeeper testified that she told him she'd never seen either suspect. He recalled the conversation at trial:

> I said to her, "Hello, Lola," and she stopped and she answered me. While she answered me I said, "You look kind of tired." She says, "Yes." She says, "They are bothering the life out of me." I says, "What?" She says, "I just come from jail." I says, "What have you done in jail?" She says, "The Government took me down and want me to recognize those men." she says, "and I don't know a

thing about them. I have never seen them and I can't recognize them." She says,
"Unfortunately I have been down there to get a job and I have seen many men
that I don't know and I have never paid any attention to anyone."[3]

Another witness who positively identified Vanzetti testified that he "thought at the first glance that the man was a Portuguese fellow named Tony."[4]

Frankfurter said that many of these positive identifications were rooted in the faulty police lineup—or actually the lack of any lineup at all. Normally, police have witnesses try to identify suspects from a lineup of similar-looking men or women, but in this case, the police brought in only Sacco and Vanzetti and asked witnesses if they had seen the men at or near the robbery.

Other key evidence brought to trial was the way Sacco and Vanzetti lied to police after being arrested. This type of behavior is known as the consciousness of guilt. But the men may have been acting guilty because they actually were guilty of what they believed they were arrested for: being anarchists. With both eyewitness accounts and the defendants' guilty behavior being questionable evidence, the more scientific firearm analysis was especially important in this case.

Sacco and Vanzetti both owned guns. Sacco said it was because he was a night watchman at the shoe factory, and Vanzetti claimed his was for self-defense (he testified that as a fishmonger, he at times carried $100 or so, $1,000 today). Sacco owned a .32-caliber Colt automatic. Vanzetti owned a .38-caliber revolver. Six bullets were found in the dead bodies. One came from a .32-caliber Colt automatic like Sacco's gun. The other five came from neither type of gun.

Captain William Proctor of the Massachusetts State Police was the expert witness for the prosecution. When he testified that the bullet had come from the same type of .32-caliber Colt that Sacco owned, the prosecutor told the jury that this meant that the bullet came from Sacco's gun. But after the trial, Proctor explained that he never found evidence that the bullet had come from Sacco's specific gun, only a gun like his. "Had I been asked the direct question: Whether I had found any affirmative evidence whatever that this so-called mortal bullet had passed through this particular Sacco's pistol, I should have answered then, as I do now without hesitation, in the negative," he said.[5] But the differentiation was too late. Sacco and Vanzetti had been found guilty, and no new trial would be granted.

In a final twist, while Sacco and Vanzetti were appealing the verdict, another man confessed to the crime. Celestino F. Madeiros was in prison for bank robbery when he passed a note to Sacco through the jail messenger; it read, "I hear by confess to being in the South Braintree and Sacco and Vanzetti was not in said crime."[6]

Madeiros said he was confessing out of a sense of guilt: "I seen Sacco's wife come up here with the kids and I felt sorry for the kids," he said.[7] His role in the supposed plot had been minor: he'd sat in the backseat as a sort of lookout for the more experienced gang members. He refused to name the others who had participated, but investigators believed it to be the Morelli gang, a group accused of stealing freight from trains in Braintree.

Several parts of Madeiros's story made sense. One gang member, Joe Morelli, had a Colt .32 at the time, and while in prison for another crime he had apparently asked a fellow prisoner to give him an alibi for April 15, 1920. Another gang member, a man named

Mancini, owned a gun that matched the other bullets found on the bodies. Madeiros also had $2,800 in the bank, which would have been his even share of the loot. Moreover, the account jibed with the feeling some investigators had that the robbery was carried out not by an anarchist fish peddler and a shoe factory worker, but by professional criminals who knew what they were doing.

On the other hand, Madeiros got some details wrong about the case. For instance, he said the money was in a bag, when it was really in boxes. He also couldn't accurately describe the neighborhood where the crime occurred. Investigators who looked into the confession believed Madeiros was just blowing smoke. True, he gained nothing from the confession, but he didn't really lose anything either. After all, he didn't confess to the murder or theft, merely to being there.

Sacco and Vanzetti were denied all motions for a new trial, and on April 9, 1927, they were sentenced to death amid worldwide protests. As a result of the protests, Massachusetts Governor A. T. Fuller appointed a commission to determine if Sacco and Vanzetti should be freed. The commission recommended that the convictions be upheld. Soon after, Goddard offered to test the bullets. He fired rounds from Sacco's gun and compared the shells and bullets to those found at the scene. Interestingly, he found that one shell and one bullet matched the gun. A 1961 panel of forensic firearm experts confirmed the same thing.

Does that mean the men were guilty? Some insiders believed only one man to be. Carlo Tresa, an anarchist leader who was originally set to defend the men in trial, said in 1943, "Sacco was guilty, but Vanzetti was innocent."[8] Another member of the defense team said,

"Sacco was guilty. . . . Vanzetti was innocent as far as the actual participation in killing."[9] Even the prosecution may have believed only one of the men to have been guilty. Vanzetti's guilty verdict reportedly brought the assistant prosecutor to tears.

In 2005, a letter turned up containing new information about the Sacco and Vanzetti case. It was penned in 1929 by Upton Sinclair, famed author of *The Jungle*. In the letter, Sinclair told his lawyer about the turmoil he felt while writing his new novel, *Boston*, a fictionalized account of the Sacco and Vanzetti trial. While researching the novel, he heard shocking information from defense attorney Fred Moore: that both men were guilty and that the defense team fabricated their alibis. Sinclair decided that the information was unreliable. (He suspected that Moore was on drugs and knew that Moore had had a bitter falling out with the rest of the defense team. Sinclair also learned from Moore's ex-wife that during the trial, he had said he thought the men were innocent.) From others in the anarchist community, Sinclair heard conflicting reports: that both men were guilty, that neither was, and that Sacco alone was. Sinclair stayed the course in writing the novel as if the men were innocent, though clearly he had his doubts. If it was true that Sacco, at least, bore the guilt, then the firearm analysis—linking Sacco's gun to the bullets found at the scene—told the real story of what happened in Braintree that day, or part of it, anyway.

Goddard weighed in on another sensational murder case of the 1920s: the gangland shooting known as the St. Valentine's Day Massacre. In 1929, gun violence was rampant in Chicago. The town was run by the mob, and the mob was run by Al Capone. Prohibition had been good for Capone and other organized crime leaders. Though

making, distributing, and selling alcohol were outlawed in 1920, all
these things were still happening through the practice of bootlegging. And because bootleggers were outside the law, they didn't have
to follow any rules. They could take over as many distilleries, brew-
eries, and bars as they wanted without it being called a monopoly.
And rather than negotiating, like normal people, they could simply
kill anyone who stood in their way. This no-holds-barred style of
business was extremely lucrative. Capone's illegal enterprises were
estimated to earn $100 million a year. Some of the profits from
bootlegging went toward bribing police and politicians so that the
illegal businesses wouldn't be shut down. These alliances made gangs
even more powerful. Prohibition was such a boon to organized crime
that leaders even held a national convention in 1928. Twenty-three
crime bosses—all from Sicilian families—met in Cleveland, Ohio,
to collaborate and share ideas. But rival gangs didn't always play nice.

Al Capone   George "Bugs" Moran

In the late 1920s, George "Bugs" Moran, leader of a North Chicago gang, began stealing shipments of bootlegged whiskey from Capone. If you were going to steal whiskey from someone, Capone probably wasn't your best target. Besides being a gangster, he was a certifiable psychopath. At one point, he beat three of his former gang members to death with a baseball bat during a company dinner. Bugs would soon know Capone's wrath.

Capone had placed a spy in Bugs's gang, and that spy arranged a shipment of stolen whiskey to be delivered to Bugs's warehouse on February 14, 1929—Valentine's Day. That morning, the Moran gangsters began arriving: Johnny May, Adam Heyer, Pete and Frank Gusenberg, James Clark, and Albert Weinshank, along with Dr. Reinhardt Schwimmer, an eye doctor who was not a gangster but was friends with the group. Weinshank looked like Bugs, and upon seeing the lookalike, Capone's men mistakenly put the plan in action before their main target had even arrived.

Capone's gangsters pulled up in a black Packard—the make of police cars at the time. Two were dressed as police officers, and two or three others wore overcoats. Bugs arrived at about the same time but, seeing what he thought was a police raid, fled the scene. His gangsters weren't so lucky. The phony police officers ordered Moran's men to line up against a brick wall and surrender their weapons. When they obeyed the orders, the gunmen pulled out their machine guns and opened fire. Capone's men then fled the scene posing as police officers making an arrest. The men wearing overcoats held their hands in the air, and the men dressed as police officers followed, guns drawn.

The real police arrived to find a bloody scene. The bodies

Chicago police reenacting the St. Valentine's Day Massacre

contained thirty-nine bullets and bullet fragments. Many more lit-
tered the floor, along with dozens of shell casings. Dr. Goddard was
brought in to analyze the firearm evidence. Goddard had his work
cut out for him. He had never seen so many bullets and shells from
a single murder scene. But he was able to draw several conclusions.
First, all the bullets and shells came from one or more .45 automatic
submachine guns. Because the casings had different markings, two
guns must have been used. The bullets had six right-twisting
grooves—the kind found in the barrel of a Thompson submachine
gun or "Tommy gun."

Goddard was able to show that the bullets didn't come from any
of the Chicago police's Tommy guns (something the public suspected
since the gangsters had posed as police officers). In spite of Goddard's analysis, the police were unable to find the matching guns,
even after several arrests. Bugs himself voluntarily came forward to

talk to the police, famously stating, "Only Capone kills like that."[10] Capone, however, had an alibi: at the time of the killings, he was being questioned by Miami police for other crimes.

Officials examining machine guns thought to be used in the St. Valentine's Day Massacre

Then, ten months later, a man named Fred Burke was involved in a traffic accident in Michigan. While being escorted to the police station, he shot and killed a police officer and hijacked a car, which he later abandoned. Documents in the car led police to Burke's home. There, officers found two Tommy guns that Goddard was able to link to the St. Valentine's Day Massacre. Burke was finally captured in the spring of 1930, but instead of being tried for the Chicago shoot-up, he was tried in Michigan for the murder of the police officer and sentenced to life. Another suspect in the killing, Jack McGurn, was killed by machine-gun fire by rival gangsters in 1936.

As for the gang leaders, Al Capone was never brought to trial for his violent crimes, but he was convicted of tax evasion in 1931. Upon his release, he was suffering from syphilis and too sick to regain his power. Bugs Moran was later convicted of bank robbery and died in prison. Goddard, on the other hand, got a happy ending. Hearing about his work on the case, wealthy philanthropists donated money to fund a new lab for him: the Scientific Crime Detection Laboratory at Northwestern University.

By 1930, firearm analysis was common in criminal cases. Oftentimes, the type of bullet found at the crime scene pointed to a certain type of suspect. A woman leaving a Brooklyn movie theater in June of 1937 suddenly collapsed. She said to her husband, "John, I think I've been shot."[11] An ambulance arrived and found a gunshot wound. At first, the police suspected gangsters. Her husband was a contractor, and the construction business had been infiltrated by gangs.

It worked like this: a gangster would join a union and work his way into a leadership position. Then he would steal from union members' salaries, dues, and pensions. Needless to say, this must have infuriated union members, but they couldn't exactly speak up—the gang's complaint department had guns. In other cases, union leaders formed alliances with gangs so that they could strong-arm employers for better wages. When Prohibition was repealed in 1933, bootleggers were no longer needed, and so gangs shifted their focus more heavily to racketeering. For this reason, the police thought organized crime might have been involved in the shooting, and that the real target was John, not his wife.

But the police discovered that the deadly bullet came from a .22-caliber small rifle—hardly the type of gun associated with organized crime. Gangsters preferred heavy-caliber weapons. (Caliber refers to the size of the gun barrel. A .22 rifle has a diameter of approximately 22/100 of an inch and is considered low-caliber. A .38 and a .45 have diameters of approximately 38/100 and 45/100 of an inch, respectively, and are high-caliber.) A .22 was—and still is—a rifle given to young people who are just learning to shoot. The entrance wound suggested that the shot had been fired from the tenements across the street. Police searched every apartment and finally found an eighteen-year-old with a .22. He'd been aiming at the lightbulbs on the theater marquee and tragically misfired.

A .38 was a common weapon among gangsters, including Francis "Two Gun" Crowley, one of many gangsters whose careers flourished during Prohibition. His string of violent crimes was traceable by the bullets found at the crime scenes, though he himself was hard to track down. Born on Halloween of 1911, Francis was placed in the poor but loving foster home of Anne Crowley. While in her care, he came to idolize his foster brother John, who was not exactly a stellar role model.

John was constantly in trouble with the law and, as a result, had a real problem with cops. He particularly disliked Officer Maurice Harlow, who had arrested John for drunkenness and disorderliness. One night, John was at a rowdy party when the police were called, and as fate would have it, Harlow responded. John fired on Harlow, who shot back. Both men died. Francis, just thirteen at the time, blamed the police for his brother's death. He later explained that he hated cops "because they were always suspecting me, on account of my step-brother having been killed in a fight with a patrolman."[12]

Francis began stealing cars for the gangs that had become so powerful. By 1931, he was a wanted man. But when a police officer tried to arrest Francis, he opened fire, seriously injuring the officer. A preeminent firearms expert, Sergeant Harry Butts, examined the recovered bullets and said they matched those found after a gunfight at an American Legion dance. Bullets of the same type were also found on the body of Virginia Brannen, a twenty-three-year-old dance hall hostess (a job that entailed dancing with customers for ten cents a dance). Highly motivated to catch the elusive killer, police distributed a wanted poster. Police officer Fred Hirsch was carrying the poster in his pocket when he approached a suspicious-looking car parked on Black Shirt Lane. He recognized Francis behind the wheel, sitting next to his girlfriend, Helen Walsh. When Hirsch asked Francis for his license, he pretended to reach for it but grabbed his gun instead. He shot Hirsch, stole the officer's revolver, shot him again with that, and sped away. Hirsch, a father of four, was supposed to have already ended his shift but had stayed to help his younger partner.

The police told reporters that Francis had surely killed Helen, who was just sixteen, since she was a witness to the murder, but really, the two lovebirds were on the run together, along with Francis's friend Rudolph "Tough Red" Duringer. (It had actually been Tough Red who had shot Virginia with Francis's gun—he said out of jealousy, though witnesses said it was a hired hit.) Helen reassured her mother of her safety in a letter.

"Dear Mom: I'm all right and don't worry about me. I am being well taken care of. We were married today. He is taking me to Canada tonight." As to what they were doing in the car, Helen reassured her mother about that, too: "We were not petting. We were sitting there talking and Shorty was afraid that I would get shot and that's why he got away so fast."[13] The letter helped lead the police to Francis.

By now, the city was crawling with cops and reporters wanting a piece of Francis. His options for hideouts were limited. Still, he probably could have done better than to ask his recently jilted girlfriend for help. But that's exactly what he did. He moved himself, Helen, and Tough Red into the apartment of Irene "Billie" Dunne, who Francis had recently dumped to go out with Helen. Billie apparently tipped off the police, and soon, Officers Dominick Caso and William Mara arrived at her West Nineteenth Street apartment. A note on her door said she'd gone out shopping, but it was clear that someone was home. The officers called for backup, and several detectives arrived. Francis must have heard the commotion, because he fired through the door and walls of the apartment. More backup was called in.

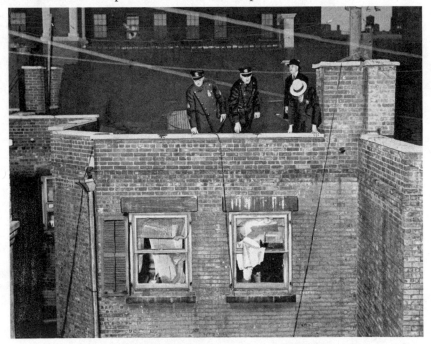

Detectives on the roof of the apartment where Francis Crowley and two others were caught by police

Soon, 150 officers were gathered in the streets below the apartment. Francis fired at them from the window while Helen and Tough Red took turns hiding under the bed. Officers and onlookers alike dodged bullets by diving behind cars. The officers returned fire, and debris fell from the building as it was peppered with bullets. A team of officers climbed onto the roof, cut a hole in the ceiling, and threw tear gas into the apartment. But Francis hurled the gas canisters into the street and opened fire at the officers through the ceiling. By now, the bad guys were running low on ammunition.

Fearing the end, Francis wrote a semi-rhyming, semi-coherent note explaining his violent rampage.

> *To whom it may concern:*
>
> *I was born on the thirty-first. She was born on the thirteenth. I guess it was fate that made us mate. When I die put a lily in my hand, let the boys know how they'll look. Underneath my coat will lay a wary kind heart what wouldn't harm anything. I hadn't nothing else to do. That's why I went around bumping off cops. It's the new sensation of the films. Take a tip from me to never let a copper go an inch above your knee. They will tell you they love you but as soon as you turn your back they will club you and say "the hell with you." Now that my death is so near there is a couple of bulls at the door and saying "come hear." I'm behind the door with three thirty-eights one which belongs to my friend who put on weight so quick in North Merrick. He would have gotten me if his bullets were any good.[14]*

The last reference was to Officer Hirsch, who apparently had shot back at Francis but had a faulty pistol and so missed. "Put on weight" referred to the weight of the lead bullets.

The police were anxious to bring the shootout to an end. A crowd of 10,000 had gathered to watch and were breaking through the police barriers. Neighbors in the building were leaning out their windows to see the action. The police worried someone would be shot. As Francis threw another round of tear gas canisters out the window, police hit him with machine-gun fire. Confident that he had been wounded, they stormed the apartment. When they broke down the door, Helen was crouched in the corner and Tough Red was not very toughly hiding under the bed. Francis still stood, but said, "I'm shot. I give up. Anyway, you didn't kill me." He was apparently out of ammunition and had been shot three times—on the legs and arm. In the ambulance, police found two pistols strapped to his legs. He'd planned to shoot his way out of the ambulance. He was sentenced to death, saying before his execution, "My last wish is to send my love to my mother."[15] Too bad that love didn't extend to the rest of humankind.

Today, guns and career criminals still go hand in hand. There is an ongoing case in which bullets found at the scene match the gun of a hired hit man. He has even confessed to the shooting. But a man claiming to be innocent is imprisoned instead—all because of what appears to have been a false confession. Davontae Sanford, a fourteen-year-old with a learning disability, was prone to making up stories—a trait that would have tragic implications. At around one a.m. on a September night in 2007, Detroit police responded to a call on Runyon Street, where four people had been shot and killed.

Davontae lived nearby and walked over to see the commotion. He struck up a conversation with a police officer, first telling him he knew who the shooter was and then telling them that it was his friends. The police took Davontae to the station for questioning. His mother,

Taminko Sanford, thought Davontae would only be sharing information, and so she stayed home. But Davontae was actually in a vulnerable position. Studies show that both young people and people with cognitive disabilities are more susceptible to making false confessions. Indeed, after a long night of being questioned without a parent or lawyer, Davontae himself had confessed to the crime. His defense attorney then convinced Taminko that her son should accept a plea agreement. Taminko recalls being told that without the plea, Davontae would face life in prison. "My baby never wanted to take the plea," Taminko said. "He kept telling me, momma, no, momma, no. I forced Davontae to take that plea. He was—he got thirty-seven to ninety years."[16]

Davontae Sanford confessed to killing four people in Detroit, a crime he likely did not commit.

And he didn't do it. At least, not according to Vincent Smothers, a professional hit man who claims to be the real shooter. An honor student who hung out with the "good kids," Vincent was an unlikely hit man. His parents kept him and his siblings on the straight and narrow, even in the midst of rampant crime in the neighborhood.

Then two family tragedies struck—his sister was accidentally shot to death in front of the Smotherses' home, and Vincent's father died of cancer. Around that time, Vincent began dabbling in crime. Though he got a job making air conditioning and heating ducts, he also stole cars on the side. He then tried a more lucrative but dangerous sideline: robbing drug dealers. That led him to a powwow with some big-time drug sellers, who hired him to be a hit man. He was ruthless, once killing an elderly bus driver at his employer's command. But in some ways, Vincent was still the responsible person he was raised to be. He married a nurse and had two daughters.

Vincent Smothers, a professional hit man who claims to be the real Runyon Street shooter

The Runyon Street hit, which targeted a marijuana dealer but also included three houseguests, was among Vincent's last. About a month later, the police arrested him. The jig was up. An informer had told them about Vincent's illicit profession. Now, he told police he didn't care about himself. He just wanted to keep his wife out of prison. (She was in trouble for stashing some of his weapons.) So he confessed to all his killings, including the Runyon Street murders.

That one stopped the police in their tracks. They already had a guy for that shooting. But Vincent stuck to his confession, describing the killing in vivid detail. It may seem like a case of one person's word against another's. But Davontae had since retracted his confession. And in addition to Vincent's confession, firearm evidence pointed to him as the killer. Cartridge casings and bullets found at the scene matched a .45-caliber gun and an AK-47 linked to Vincent.

Vincent was sure that his confession would free Davontae. When the two happened to run into each other in prison, Vincent assured the young man that he would be out soon. But that didn't happen. Davontae's new lawyer heard about the confession and requested an innocence trial. But Vincent refused to testify. He did file a detailed affidavit stating his role in the killings and saying that Davontae was not an accomplice. In 2014, the Michigan Supreme Court said that though Davontae couldn't undo his guilty plea, he could pursue an appeal.

Then, in June of 2015—nearly eight years after Davontae was arrested and Vincent subsequently confessed to the crime—the Wayne County Prosecutor's Office asked state police to reinvestigate. About a year later, they issued arrest warrants in the case for Vincent Smothers and an accomplice, Ernest Davis, both of whom are serving prison terms for other murders. They also sought perjury charges against a Detroit police official. Since it is virtually unthinkable that Vincent would have allowed Davontae—who he did not even know at the time—to tag along on a murder job, signs point to Davontae being freed very soon. Meanwhile, Detroit police are investigating their detectives' handling of the case. The case shows how forensic evidence can shed light on a false confession. Sadly, it also shows how confessions can be coerced, and how difficult it is to undo such a confession once it's been made.

Since its emergence in the 1920s, firearm analysis has helped to solve some of the most important cases in America, and it's no wonder, with guns being the weapon of choice for so many criminals. It will be interesting to see if, as with poisonings, stricter laws will be passed in an effort to reduce gun deaths.

ACCIDENT OR FAKED ACCIDENT?

New York Medical Examiner Dr. M. Edward Marten received news the evening of July 4, 1937, that a middle-aged woman had been shot and killed. Her distraught husband explained that at five thirty p.m., he had pulled a gun out from under a couch cushion and told his wife he intended to fire it into the air for Independence Day. She told him he would do no such thing. Mad at her for ruining his fun in the name of stupid old gun safety, he threw the weapon, still in its holster, onto the couch, and in the process tragically proved his wife right.

Immediately, she cried, "I'm shot."[17] As he walked her into the bedroom to lay her on the bed, she collapsed onto the floor. He ran and cried out for help and then returned to his wife's side. Two men came running and found the husband on the floor, kissing the wife and saying, "I killed her! I killed her."[18]

Marten had to decide whether the story was true. Examining the body, he determined that the time of death coincided with the husband calling for help (leaving no time for him to have staged the accident). The hole in the holster showed that the gun had fired while in the holster. Added to that, the entry wound suggested that the bullet trajectory had come from the couch cushion, an awkward angle from which to purposely shoot someone. Marten concluded that the husband was not guilty of murder—only carelessness.

7

Blood Is Thicker:
The First Blood Pattern Cases

Blood pattern analysis actually dates back to ancient times, when in 72 CE in Rome, the father of a blind boy was found murdered. Bloody handprints were found along the stairway leading away from the body, as though the boy had been feeling his way along the wall. But the handprints were too perfect. Investigators said the prints should have faded as the boy got farther from the scene. Instead, they remained as bright as a children's handprint mural. To appear as they did, the boy would have had to have redipped his hands in the blood. He hadn't, but his stepmother had. She was determined to have killed the man and framed the boy.

In modern times, at least in America, blood pattern analysis wasn't done in earnest until the 1950s. Then it played a major role in the Marilyn Sheppard murder investigation, a sensational case that inspired the television show and movie *The Fugitive*. Marilyn and

Samuel Sheppard were beautiful, young, and rich. They lived in Bay Village, a suburb outside of Cleveland. Sam was a doctor at the Bay View Hospital, along with his father and two brothers. Marilyn had been Sam's high school sweetheart, and together they had a son, Sam Reese Sheppard, nicknamed Chip. From the outside, it looked like the Sheppards had a perfect life, but in fact their marriage was unhappy, the details of which would come out during the trial.

Dr. Sam Sheppard and his wife, Marilyn

Early on the morning of July 4, 1954, Sam Sheppard called his friend Spencer Houk, saying, "For God's sake, Spen, get over here quick. I think they've killed Marilyn."[1]

Spencer and his wife, Esther, drove to the house, where they found Sam in the den, looking dazed. Houk asked what happened, and Sam said, "I don't know. I just remember waking up on the couch and I heard Marilyn screaming and I started up the stairs and somebody or something clobbered me and the next thing I remember was coming to down on the beach."[2]

Esther ran upstairs and back down, saying, "Call the police, call an ambulance, call everything."[3]

Patrolman Fred F. Drenkhan responded to the call at about six a.m. He found Sam slouched in a chair in the study, wearing slacks but no shirt, his face swollen and discolored. Esther told Drenkhan to see about Marilyn upstairs. The officer found her badly beaten, the bed soaked in blood, the walls splashed in red. Seven-year-old Chip was still sound asleep, and the family dog, Koko, was quiet.

Drenkhan asked Sam what happened, and he repeated the same story he had told the Houks. Drenkhan further investigated the scene. There was no sign of a forced entry. The doors of a desk in the study had been removed and lay on the floor. In the living room, the drawers of a desk were pulled open and papers strewn about. However, nothing of value appeared to have been taken. Drenkhan radioed for a doctor and the chief of police. Soon, a detective from the Cleveland Police and the Cuyahoga County coroner, Sam Gerber, also arrived.

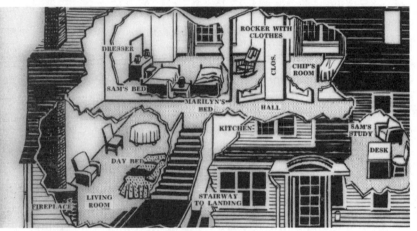

Sketch of the Sheppards' house, which was used in the murder trial

After examining the body, observing the crime scene, and speaking to Sam, Gerber told a detective, "It's obvious that the doctor did it."[4] Gerber's autopsy would reveal that Marilyn received thirty-five blows—many of them strong enough to have been fatal. Her teeth had been chipped during the attack. Though her pajamas had been partially pulled off, there were no signs of rape. She was also four months pregnant.

Sam's brothers took him to Bay Side Hospital to be treated for neck and head injuries. But detectives believed the injuries to be self-inflicted, and they made it clear that Sam was the prime suspect. Detective Robert Schottke said, "I don't know about my partner, but I think you killed your wife."[5]

The press was of the same opinion. Newspapers called for Sam's arrest. An editorial in the July 30 *Cleveland Press* criticized investigators for letting Sheppard's well-connected family and friends protect him:

> *This man is a suspect in his wife's murder. Nobody yet has found a solitary trace of the presence of anybody else in his Lake Road house the night or morning his wife was brutally beaten to death in her bedroom.*
>
> *And yet no murder suspect in the history of this County has been treated so tenderly, with such infinite solicitude for his emotions, with such fear of upsetting the young man.*
>
> *Gentlemen of Bay Village, Cuyahoga County, and Cleveland, charged jointly with law enforcement—*
>
> *This is murder. This is no parlor game.*[6]

Sam was eventually arrested and put on trial. He was represented by attorney Bill Corrigan, whose strategy was to let Sam testify and hope that the jury would believe him. Sam told the jury the same strange story that he had told his friends when they arrived at the scene. He had been asleep in the den when he heard his wife cry out. He awoke and, in his own words:

> *As I went upstairs and into the room I felt that I could visualize a form of some type with a light top. As I tried to go to Marilyn I was intercepted or*

*grappled. As I tried to shake loose or strike, I felt that I was struck from behind
and my recollection was cut off. The next thing I remember was coming to a
very vague sensation in a sitting position right next to Marilyn's bed, facing the
hallway, facing south. I recall vaguely recognizing my wallet.*[7]

He was questioned as to what happened after that:

*A. Well, I realized that I had been hurt and as I came to some sort of conscious-
ness, I looked at my wife.*

Q. What did you see?

*A. She was in very bad condition. She had been—she had been badly beaten. I
felt that she was gone. And I was immediately fearful for Chip. I went into
Chip's room and in some way evaluated that he was all right. I don't know
how I did it. I, at this time or shortly thereafter, heard a noise downstairs.*

Q. And what did you do when you heard the noise downstairs?

*A. And I—I can't explain my emotion, but I was stimulated to chase or get
whoever or whatever was responsible for what had happened. I went down
the stairs, went into the living room, over toward the east portion of the living
room and visualized a form.*[8]

Sam went on to describe an altercation on the beach, during
which he was again knocked out by the "form," which he said he now
saw had bushy hair. He awoke with his body partially underwater
and went back to the house to check on Marilyn. Seeing that she'd
been badly beaten, he paced around the house, confused and horri-
fied. Finally, he called Spencer Houk.

Sam's story must have seemed suspicious to the jury. For one
thing, his description of the intruder was incredibly vague. He called

the intruder "a form of some type with a light top" and "someone or something"—as though he had no idea whether it was a person or— what? A bear? An extraterrestrial? The prosecution told the jury that neither the evidence nor the rules of time and logic matched Sam's story. If he had run upstairs as soon as he heard Marilyn cry out, only to find that the attack was complete when he reached the room, then that would mean that the attacker had managed to land thirty-five blows while Sheppard ran upstairs. The prosecution also argued that there were no signs of a struggle—either in the bedroom or on the beach. The killer would have been bloodied from the attack, and so blood would have transferred to Sheppard and then onto the floor and ground. But no such bloodstains were found in these places.

Dr. Sam Sheppard on trial
for the murder of his wife

There *was* blood found on Sheppard's watch—tiny droplets consistent with the blood that sprays during an attack. If Sheppard had been wearing it when examining his wife after the attack, it should have been smeared instead. In other words, when compared to Sam's story, there was blood where it shouldn't be, and there wasn't blood where it should be. The prosecution also presented more speculative blood evidence. Gerber, the coroner, said that he'd found on the pillow a bloodstain that looked like it was the result of a tool being laid down. He theorized that it was a surgical instrument—and the murder weapon.

In addition to blood evidence, the prosecutor focused on Sheppard's private life. A former coworker of Sheppard's, Susan Hayes, testified that she'd been having an affair with Sheppard for some time. Marilyn was revealed to be unhappy in the marriage for other reasons, too. She had told Houk that Sam was "a Jekyll and a Hyde."[9] After deliberating for several days, the jury found Sheppard guilty, and he was sent to a maximum security prison. But the story didn't end there.

In 1955, Corrigan hired criminalist Dr. Paul Kirk to analyze the crime scene. Kirk focused on the scene of the attack: the bedroom. He said that, looking at the blood spatter on the walls in the room, there was a space where there was little blood. This would have been blocked by the killer. He argued that the killer would have been covered in blood, not just have a stain on the knee of his pants, as Dr. Sheppard had. Kirk also debunked Gerber's theory that the weapon was a surgical instrument. He ran blood spatter tests, akin to those now seen on the show *Dexter*, and determined the weapon to be a flashlight. (A neighbor of the Sheppards' found a flashlight in Lake Erie near the home around the same time.) Kirk said that the mark on the pillow could have come from the pillowcase being wrinkled at that spot—as opposed to a surgical instrument being laid there. He further theorized that the killer was left-handed, whereas Sam was right-handed. Finally, Kirk said that the chipped teeth found with the body meant that Marilyn had probably bitten the killer's hand, and the killer would have bled. Kirk said that he found type O blood on the scene that was different from Marilyn's type O blood. He concluded that it must be from the bleeding hand, and that the killer must have type O blood, whereas Sam had type A blood.

A judge said that Corrigan had been free to present this analysis at the first trial, and so no new trial was granted. Corrigan died shortly after the appeal, and Sheppard hired a new attorney, F. Lee Bailey. Bailey argued that the guilty verdict should be overturned based on the fact that the press coverage cast a negative light on Sheppard, denying him the right to a fair trial. The appeal made it all the way to the US Supreme Court, which agreed that the "carnival atmosphere"[10] of the trial potentially prejudiced the jury. The conviction was overturned.

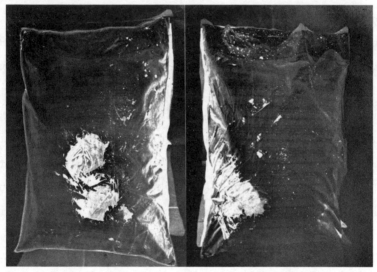

Both sides of the bloodstained pillow on which Marilyn Sheppard was murdered

The State of Ohio tried Sheppard again in 1966. This time, Bailey was able to use Kirk's expert testimony. Public opinion had also changed. A popular TV show, *The Fugitive*, reflected remarkable similarities to Sam's account of the murder. *The Fugitive*'s title character, Dr. Richard Kimble, was also a doctor accused of murdering his wife. He had seen the real attacker, in this case a one-armed man, not the bushy-haired form that Sam described. Kimble had escaped federal custody and was now trying to track down the real killer. Bailey himself seemed aware of *The Fugitive*'s possible positive effect on the jury; he asked them if they'd heard of the show.

But instead of having Sam testify, Bailey kept his client off the stand. The attorney presented a rather outlandish new theory as to who the true killer could be. He said that Marilyn was having an affair with Spencer Houk and that it was his wife, Esther, who'd killed Marilyn. Because Sam didn't testify, prosecutors couldn't cross-examine him about the bushy-haired form he'd reported seeing, which conflicted with the new theory. Sam was found not guilty and released. A grand jury never indicted Esther Houk. Sam became a professional wrestler known as Killer Sheppard, and in 1970, he died. But that wasn't the end of the story either.

In 1996, Marilyn and Sam Sheppard's son, Sam Reese Sheppard (previously nicknamed Chip), brought a case against the State of Ohio for the malicious prosecution and wrongful imprisonment of his father. He and his attorney, Terry Gilbert, had a new theory regarding who committed the murder. They blamed a window washer who had worked for the Sheppards, Richard Eberling. Whereas Esther Houk was a rather unlikely suspect, Richard actually had a checkered past. In 1989, he was convicted of murdering Ethel Durkin, an elderly woman in his care, and forging her will to make himself a beneficiary. Richard wrote a letter to Sam Reese from prison saying he knew who really killed Marilyn. He said it was Esther Houk, and that her husband and Sam covered it up. Sam Reese wanted to clear his father's name, but he didn't believe the Esther Houk story. He thought Richard might have done it. And there was some evidence pointing to that. For instance, an acquaintance of Richard's said that he had confessed to murdering Marilyn. The plaintiffs also said that blood found on the scene matched Richard's DNA. Richard died before the civil case went to trial.

To fight the civil case, the State of Ohio brought in former FBI profiler Gregg McCrary to analyze the original murder case. Like the original investigators, McCrary was struck by the lack of blood found in certain areas of the scene. Sam said he had wrestled with the killer twice, and the killer had to have been soaked with blood. But there was no evidence of a bloody brawl having taken place. There was also no blood on the desk, even though the killer had supposedly rummaged through it. There was no evidence of the killer washing up prior to ransacking the house, and had he ransacked it prior to killing Marilyn and knocking out Sam, Sam surely would have woken up, as he had been sleeping nearby.

McCrary also looked at the case using a strategy known as victimology. The investigator asks what increased the victim's likelihood of being murdered. This can lead to the motive, and then the suspect. For instance, if the victim was a drug dealer, that high-risk profession may have led to his or her murder. The culprit may have murdered to steal drugs, or as retribution for stolen drugs. But Marilyn didn't have a high-risk lifestyle. The only thing that made her more likely to be a victim was her volatile marriage. There was even evidence that she was planning on getting back at her husband for his unfaithfulness. Friends of hers told police that weeks before the murder, Marilyn had said she would "divorce him, ruin him financially, and drag his name through the mud."[11] The fact that Sam was present during the murder made him all the more suspicious.

McCrary then went through a list of red flags that indicated crime scene staging (that is, altering the crime scene to confuse police).

1. The stronger person is injured minimally, whereas the weaker person suffers grave injuries. Sam was bigger than Marilyn and posed a greater threat to an intruder. But the killer beat Marilyn to death, and only knocked Sam out.
2. If the motive was supposed to be robbery, inappropriate items are taken. Though the desk and dresser had been rifled through, the killer took nothing of value.
3. The crime is made to look like rape, but there is no evidence of rape. Marilyn's pajama top had been pulled up and the bottoms had been pulled down, suggesting rape, but no rape had occurred.
4. The murder involves overkill—more violence than was needed to cause death—very true in this case.
5. It is arranged for someone else to discover the dead body. Sam called his friends to come "see about Marilyn."
6. The crime scene is the victim's or offender's home—also true in this case.

During the trial, McCrary was unable to state that he believed Sam had killed his wife. When a verdict hinges on one question, experts aren't allowed to answer that question (which is known as the ultimate issue). However, McCrary *could* testify that the evidence pointed to a staged domestic homicide, and that's exactly what he did. Meanwhile, the DNA evidence pointing to Richard Eberling proved to be a bust. The blood that was to be tested against his DNA wasn't even the right blood type. Both Richard and Sam were type A. The blood sample was type O—Marilyn's type. (Kirk's original tests showing two different kinds of type O blood on the scene have since been determined to be unreliable.) The jury found for the State of Ohio, meaning that Sam Sheppard was still considered guilty in the eyes of the law. And *that* was the end of the story. At least for now.

The Marilyn Sheppard case showed that whereas the suspect may tell one story, there is another written in blood. In other cases, blood patterns reveal that the suspect is actually telling the truth. On January 5, 1964, criminalist Larry Ragle was called to a mansion in Newport Beach, California. The owner, William Bartholomae, had struck it rich panning for gold, drilling for oil, and ranching. But he'd recently met his end—stabbed to death in his own kitchen.

William's body had been taken to the hospital, along with two women who had survived the events of the day. Ragle learned that along with William, his brother Charles; Charles's wife, Carmen; and the couple's new baby lived at the house. In addition, Carmen's sister Minola Gallardo was visiting from Spain to help with the baby. Carmen had felt poorly since giving birth and was seeing a doctor for nausea, dizziness, and blackouts. Carmen and Minola were the two women taken to the hospital.

The housemates had planned a morning cruise on William's yacht, the *Sea Diamond*, but strong winds prevented them from setting sail. According to Ragle's account, William was angry about the canceled trip, and everyone was trying to stay out of his way. Minola went upstairs to take care of the baby. Soon after, something went horribly wrong.

Ragle found blood on the kitchen floor, but not as much as might be expected after a stabbing. He also found a knife blade, the handle broken off. He followed a trail of blood out the door, across the lawn, and to the *Sea Diamond*, where the droplets stopped short of the gangplank. That told Ragle the blood trail belonged to someone reluctant to get blood on the boat. The captain was still on the *Sea Diamond*. He said Charles had been helping him shut down the equipment when Minola came to the foot of the gang plank yelling, *"Ayuda! Ayuda!"* ("Help! Help!")[12] Her hands were bleeding, and the captain called the police.

Ragle spoke to Charles, who explained that both women spoke only Spanish. They were afraid of William, who spoke no Spanish and was gruff with them. Charles told the sisters that William's bark was worse than his bite, but they apparently didn't believe him. (Though later, Carmen was quoted in an Associated Press article: "He was such a good man. He was so good to Charles and me.")[13]

William's autopsy revealed the cause of death to be internal bleeding from being stabbed in the liver. He had other stab wounds, but the fatal wound must have come early on. The minimal blood found at the scene indicated that the victim died quickly, and so the heart had stopped pumping blood. If more pooled blood had been found on the scene, it would have meant that the victim lived for a while after being wounded, and so the heart kept pumping blood. Ragle also found moon-shaped cuts on William's face—possibly fingernail marks. Ragle scraped under both women's nails. Under Minola's nails, he found skin and white whiskers, likely from William. Ragle also had the blood gathered from the scene tested for type.

Based on the fingernail scrapings and blood evidence, he pieced together the story. Carmen had been doing dishes when she passed out from her postpartum illness. The knife was out because it was being washed. William came to her aid. At that moment, Minola came onto the scene and saw her sister collapsed, William kneeling over her, and a knife. She thought he had attacked Carmen. He spoke no Spanish, so he couldn't explain himself. Minola came at him from behind, prying him away from her sister and scratching his face in the process. He grabbed the knife in self-defense and cut her hands. He didn't really want to hurt Minola and so was being careful. She, on the other hand, thought she was fighting for her sister's life and fought hard. She managed to pry the knife out of William's hands. He defended himself for a while, cutting his hands in the process, but Minola managed to stab him in the liver. Minola then tried to waken Carmen, but she was still passed out, so Minola ran to the boat for help.

Minola was tried, and during the trial, the defense presented the same story Ragle had constructed based on blood evidence, only Carmen was chopping mushrooms, not washing dishes. Minola was found not guilty because her actions were legally excusable. It was all a misunderstanding. A deadly one.

In these cases, the blood was left in the open for investigators to see. But what about crime scenes that are covered up? Even then, blood can tell on people. It can never be scrubbed away—not fully. In the 1960s, new forensic science tools helped investigators see blood invisible to the naked eye. A man in Germany found that out the hard way.

Friedrich Lindörfer lived in a small house in Reichelshofen, Germany, with his wife, two grown sons, a daughter, her husband, their children, and his fifty-two-year-old sister Lina. Lina had a hip disease, and so when Friedrich's parents gave him the family home, they made him promise to let his sister live there as long as she wanted, which he did, begrudgingly. One spring day in 1962, Lina's friend Anna Eckel came to visit. Lina wasn't home but had left food and sewing on the table in her room, which was strange because Lina was a neat freak. The lock on her door was also broken. Friedrich walked by and glared at Anna, and so she left.

Anna had misgivings about her friend's absence, and so she went to a neighbor's house to talk. The neighbor hadn't seen Lina leave the house and thought the whole thing odd. The neighbor marched over and asked Friedrich where Lina was. He explained that she had gotten in a car with a man he didn't know. He accused Anna of breaking the lock. She didn't take that accusation lightly and went to the police to accuse Friederich of slander. The police had received complaints earlier from Lina that her brother was trying to drive her away. So they told Friederich that he needed to track down his sister and let them know she was okay. When the police learned that Lina hadn't turned up anywhere, they began investigating her disappearance as a possible murder.

By now, several days had passed. They searched the Lindörfer house but came up short on evidence. Then, on August 23, an Inspector Heberger arrived with a special lamp to detect blood. Though no blood was found, Friederich's nervousness during the procedure suggested to Heberger that he was on the right track. He called the Institute of Forensic Medicine in Erlangen, leaders in the field of serology, the study of blood. A scientist named Lautenbach agreed to investigate.

Heberger got another search warrant and went to the house at night, when the results would be clearer. Lautenbach sprayed luminol, a chemical used to detect the presence of blood, and then searched the house with a flashlight. If blood was present, the area would emit a blue glow. Lautenbach searched places where a body would be dragged—over steps, thresholds, and floors—and places a murderer would touch—door handles, latches, and faucets. The steps didn't glow, but they had recently been painted. Lina's room was also blood-free. But the door leading to the attic glowed. Inside, there was more glowing blue—on a large floorboard, a pile of charcoal, some cardboard, an ax, and a shoe tree. Some of the objects were taken to the lab so that they could be tested for blood type (Lina was type A). But Lautenbach couldn't get a good read, and before he could do more testing, the district attorney dropped the case for lack of evidence.

The case was reopened when a new inspector, Valentin Freund, came on the job. He was examining cold cases and thought more blood testing could have been done in the Lindörfer case. He returned to the home on April 9, 1963, and though much of the original evidence was gone, he found a pair of women's shoes with brown stains. These were tested and came up showing type-A blood. Lautenbach returned, spraying the attic with a higher-powered luminol spray gun. Now he could see even more bloodstains. It was clear that somebody with type-A blood had been injured—or killed—in the attic.

Lautenbach and Freund built a wooden model of the attic, labeling all the areas where blood was found. Based on this, the district attorney arrested Friederich. Freund interrogated the man for two days, but Friederich stuck to his story: his sister had driven off with a stranger. On the third day, however, Friederich added, "It will all come to light. Everything does," [14] and started sobbing. Freund produced the model of the attic. Friederich stared in horror and began his confession—the first version, anyway.

He said that after lunch, his sons and son-in-law were returning to work as coopers, or barrel makers. His wife and daughter were working in the garden, and he told Lina to go help. She was ironing and said she was too busy. He said that she wasn't too busy to write anonymous letters. (Neighbors said she'd been writing anonymous letters that accused another neighbor of adultery.) The brother and sister argued. She chased him with the iron, but he grabbed it and followed her into the attic. There he threw the iron, killing her. He then buried her in a field.

Lautenbach said that the bloodstain evidence contradicted this story. The amount of spatter showed that Lina didn't die from a single blow but several. Now Friederich confessed that, in fact, Lina had locked her bedroom door during the argument, and he had broken the lock and come in. He had dragged his sister up into the attic and struck her with the iron twice. She fell, bleeding, close to the charcoal. He then dragged her body out of view of the doorway, which is how the blood got on the box, shoes, and cardboard. *Then* he buried the body.

But investigators couldn't find the body where Friederich said it would be. Friederich then admitted to disposing of the body in a more macabre way. He had chopped it up in the barn while the family was away and then burned it in the stove. Lautenbach confirmed that there were bloodstains in the barn, but the stove was too small to have burned the body. That's when Friederich gave his fourth and final confession. He said that, true enough, he had tried to burn the body, but it was impossible. So he boiled it in a large pot, stripped the flesh from the bones, and burned that part. He buried some of his sister's ashes in their mother's grave, out of a sense of duty (really, it was the least he could do). He then put the bones in paper bags and carried them to the woods. He emptied the water in the bushes around the home, and fat clung to the leaves, but nobody—including the police—noticed.

He said, "You never believe what a man is capable of—what you can bring yourself to do . . . but then I went to bed just like I do every day."[15]

After murdering his sister, Friederich had used every free second to scrub the blood from the stairs, barn, workshop, and attic. "I didn't see any bloodstains and still I scrubbed," he said.[16] He thought that when the police came, they wouldn't find anything. But just as God knew that Cain murdered Abel, in this case, the blood knew. And it told on Friederich.

Later, testing for blood type would give way to the much more exact science of DNA profiling, or comparing sections of DNA to determine if they belong to the same person. But at the time, blood typing was helpful for ruling people out—either as suspects or, in this case, victims. That was important because, without a body, it was difficult to prosecute a murder. After all, Lina really could have run away. But this case also shows that, for a murderer, hiding a body is difficult. Not that people don't try.

8
Grave Matters: Hidden Bodies

Corpus delicti literally means the "body of the crime." In legal terms, it means proof that a crime has been committed. Some people take this to mean that a body is needed as proof of a murder. But actually, investigators have been able to build a case for murder in the absence of a body, and though rare, "no-body" murder cases have gone to trial.

In 2009, a former police officer found guilty of murdering his wife became the sixth murderer in the state of Georgia to be convicted without a body. In this case, the evidence was compelling. Theresa Parker called her family daily. Her calls, along with her other daily transactions, stopped suddenly on the day of her disappearance. And blood was found in the trunk of her car. A history of domestic violence led the police to suspect Theresa's husband, Sam Parker. He said he'd been driving around in his truck that day, but neighbors said the vehicle had been parked in the Parkers' driveway. At the trial,

155

prosecutors illustrated how the murder might have occurred. Sam had bruises on his arms when the police first spoke to him. As a police officer, he had used a chokehold during arrests. A demonstration showed that a victim of a chokehold would grasp the arms of the attacker—and that these defensive wounds matched Sam's bruises. (Theresa's jawbone was found in 2010 by a farmer cutting corn in Chattanooga County. Investigators uncovered more of her remains in the area, which had recently had severe flooding.)

The conviction rate is actually high—88 percent in America—when a no-body case goes to trial, probably because prosecutors are so selective about the no-body cases they try. In the history of America and the US Virgin Islands, only 408 no-body murder cases have gone to trial, and none whatsoever in the state of Idaho. Even if a murder is suspected in a disappearance, without a body, investigators have no known cause of death, no known weapon, no known time of death, usually no crime scene, and therefore, few leads to go on.

But bodies don't stay hidden forever. Soccer balls go rolling into forgotten woods, dogs frolic in the underbrush, and people are curious when something looks—or smells—strange. All these random occurrences have led to the discovery of clandestine graves. And ever since medical examiners have been around, they've found ingenious ways of identifying even badly decomposed bodies and determining the time and cause of death without a crime scene.

The first case brings us back to the early decades of the New York Medical Examiner's Office and begins like an episode of *Law & Order*. On November 2, 1942, a man was walking his German shepherd in Central Park. The dog barked, and the man followed it into the tall grass. There, beneath a dogwood, he found the body of a woman who'd been strangled to death. Detectives identified the body as Louise Almodovar, a twenty-four-year-old waitress who lived with her parents, who had reported her missing the day before. (In cities, clandestine graves don't stay secret for long.) Although she had no purse or money, she still wore a gold chain around her neck, making it unlikely that robbery was the motive. Detectives zeroed in on her husband, Anibal Almodovar, who she had left five months earlier because of his womanizing. When questioned, Anibal boldly said he was glad his wife was gone. She had recently beaten up one of his girlfriends. But he denied killing her. And he had an alibi.

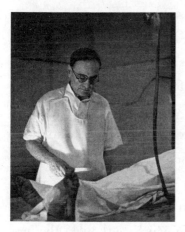

Thomas A. Gonzalez, New York City medical examiner

The New York City medical examiner, Thomas A. Gonzales, placed Louise's death between nine and ten p.m. on November 1. During that time, Anibal had been at the Rumba Palace, a dance hall, with his new girlfriend— the same one Louise had beaten up. Many people had seen him there. Anibal seemed to be out of the running for murder suspects. Then Louise's parents showed the police a threatening letter that Anibal had written to Louise. He seemed right for the crime—if it weren't for his alibi. When investigators visited the Rumba Palace, it all made sense. It was just a block or so away from the park. He could have sneaked out without anyone noticing.

Dr. Alexander Gettler worked with Gonzalez on the investigation. He noticed in the crime scene photos that the body lay in unusual grass. Earlier, grass seeds had been found in Anibal's pockets and pant cuffs. He claimed not to have set foot in Central Park for more than two years. The seeds must have come from another park. Gettler wondered whether the seeds matched the grass in Central Park, and how common that grass was. He called in Joseph Copeland, a professor of botany. Copeland said that the grasses, *Plantago lanceolata*, *Panicum dichotoflorum*, and *Eleusine indica*, grew in just one place in New York City: Central Park, and specifically, the hill where Louise was found dead. And the seeds in Anibal's pockets matched the grass.

Realizing he had failed an important botany quiz, Anibal said that he had forgotten, but he actually had walked through the park in September. It was another wrong answer. These grasses didn't go to seed until October. Anibal then confessed that he'd arranged to meet his wife in the park. They'd argued, his temper had flared, and he had killed her. He later retracted his confession but was found guilty. His wife got justice, all because of some grass seeds.

Nowadays, there are specialists in forensic botany, the study of plants to solve crimes. As with all forensic evidence, plant life can be used to verify—or contradict—a story told by a suspect. Zakaria Erzinçlioğlu, a forensic entomologist in England, described a case in his memoir, *Maggots, Murder, and Men*, in which he thought the suspect had made a false confession. William Funnell, a carpenter, was married to Anne Funnell, a bartender. Together they had three sons. Anne disappeared April 24, 1984, and her body was found eleven days later in the bushes of a public green space. William was arrested and confessed. He said that he'd been arguing with his wife for several days over a supposed affair she was having at work. On Tuesday, a fight erupted again. This time, he strangled her and left her lying in their bedroom until dark. Then he carried her body to the green.

A body that is embalmed and placed in a sealed casket can remain preserved for several decades. Contrary to the macabre children's song, when you are buried six feet under in a coffin, the worms do not crawl in, or crawl out, or play pinochle on your snout. But left in the open, a body quickly begins to rot, and smelling this, insects arrive and lay their eggs in the corpse. When hatched, the maggots and grubs feast on the flesh. The age of the maggots shows how many days the person has been dead. A forensic entomologist like Erzinçlioğlu is called in to study the maggot evidence to determine the time of death.

In this case, he observed that all the maggots were either very old or very young. That was out of the ordinary. The maggots should have varied in age, since different flies constantly lay eggs on the body. This body seemed to have been exposed to flies soon after death, then not exposed for several days, and then exposed again. In watching the video of the body's removal from the green, Erzinçlioğlu noticed something else strange. The grass underneath the body was green. As anyone who's ever had a Slip'N Slide knows, grass covered by something quickly yellows. Yet this body had supposedly been left on the green for eleven days.

Other evidence didn't match up, either. The autopsy showed that, in addition to being strangled, Anne had suffered a blow to the head that would have bled, but there were no signs of blood in the bedroom except a small stain likely caused by one of the sons' nosebleeds. Furthermore, one of the sons had gone into the bedroom after school but hadn't seen the body, which according to the confession had lain there until nightfall. (The bed was too low for the body to have been hidden underneath.) Erzinçlioğlu said that William confessed out of fear that one of his sons would be charged. Though there was no evidence against the boys, detectives had suggested that one of them would be tried if not William. So William confessed, hoping the truth would come out at trial, at which point he recanted his confession and pled innocent. As other cases in this book show, that is a dangerous assumption, and William was found guilty.

Maggots have aided investigators since 1855. That year, a couple was remodeling their home outside Paris when a body was found behind the mantel. The homeowners immediately became suspects. But they hadn't been living in the home for long, so it was important to determine when the body had been hidden. Swiss doctor Bergeret d'Arbois was called in to conduct the autopsy. To determine the time of death, he studied the maggots and mites that had infested the body. Based on their life cycles, he learned that the person had been dead for seven years. The present homeowners hadn't moved in yet. So the earlier occupants were suspected instead.

The same type of work was done sporadically through the years, but it wasn't until the 1970s and '80s that dedicated studies of insects on corpses were made. In 1987, Dr. William Bass created America's first body farm at the University of Tennessee, Knoxville. Here, donated bodies were placed outdoors so that researchers could observe how a body decomposed in the open air. This would help forensic scientists to determine time of death, which is crucial to creating a timeline, determining when the victim was last seen, and checking alibis.

Based on insects found with the corpse, forensic entomologists can also tell the season in which the death occurred. In another of

Dr. William Bass studying a decomposed body at the body farm

Erzinçlioğlu's cases, an elderly woman's body was found in October when a neighbor noticed a strong smell. The body contained several pupae, which the entomologist gathered to study under the microscope. He found five species of flies—four of which were active only in June and July. That meant the woman had been dead since summer. During that time, a man who worked for her had skipped town. Now he was a suspect. It turned out she was a domineering employer but had promised the man an inheritance when she died. He killed her for the money and fled in fear. But his very departure led investigators to him—that and those flies.

Forensic entomology helped Rockland County medical examiner Frederick Zugibe solve the Case of the Slash-Faced Woman. In October of 1984, workers at a hotel in Nanuet, New York, were playing soccer when the ball rolled into the woods. A player jogged over to get it and found the body of a woman whose face had been slashed. Maggots were in the wounds. The hotel security camera was for some reason pointed away from the parking lot. Otherwise, the killer would have been caught on tape. Instead, the case was much more difficult to solve.

The body belonged to Marie Jefferson, a thirty-two-year-old woman from the Bronx, who had been missing for a week and a half. She had last been seen in Manhattan with her ex-fiancé, Samuel McCullough. The nature of the wounds ruled out robbery. A robber kills quickly—and wouldn't take the time to slash the victim's face. Such gratuitous violence also suggested that the murderer killed out of rage. Death was caused by a stab wound to the chest, and from this incision, Zugibe determined the weapon to be a sharp blade. Because the incision showed that the sharp side of the knife was facing the right, he guessed that the killer was left-handed. (People tend to turn the knife inward.)

Because Marie had been dead for some time, Zugibe would be unable to use some of the traditional methods of determining time of death, such as observing whether rigor mortis had set in, taking the body temperature, and noting changes in the pupils. He still did a battery of tests, including checking the potassium levels in the eyeballs, which increase after death. Time of death is never as exact as it is shown on TV, but in this case, the range was six to twenty days, hardly a helpful time frame for investigators. Zugibe turned to forensic entomology to narrow it down. He gathered blowfly maggots from the wounds and also took live flies from the corpse to observe their life cycle. Based on this, he determined her to have been dead for seven to nine days.

In the meantime, investigators learned that Marie's ex had a history of violence against her and had recently been stalking and threatening her. They tracked down witnesses who had last seen her with Samuel and asked them to demonstrate how the two were walking. The witnesses showed that he had pushed her arm up behind her and led her away. The timing of these accounts matched up with the time of death the medical examiner had given. Samuel was tried and found guilty of murder. He died in prison.

Time of death was especially elusive in another case handled by Zugibe. In September 1983, a police officer spotted a woman's blouse near a stone wall on the side of the road. He got out of his car to investigate and found beside it a heavy-duty garbage bag containing what appeared to be a body. When Zugibe unwrapped what turned out to be several bags, insects poured out. Inside was the body of a middle-aged man, six feet tall, two hundred pounds, who had died from a bullet to the head. He appeared to have died three or four weeks earlier. But there were several strange things about the body.

First, usually after death, bacteria feed on the dead tissue, emitting gas as part of their digestive process. This causes the body to bloat. But that hadn't happened in this case. Second, the skin was a strange shade of beige—not normal after death. Third, the body's internal organs usually decompose first, but this body was decomposing from the outside in, with many organs still intact.

Zugibe suspected staging. The killer might have frozen the body to make it look like the murder had occurred more recently than it really had. This would account for the organs decomposing last.

Just as giblets inside a frozen turkey are the last to thaw, so would be the organs in a frozen human body. Zugibe examined cells under a microscope. Indeed, they were distorted from being frozen for months or even years.

The hands of the body were mummified, so Zugibe injected the fingertips with a chemical solution before taking prints, as in the Brooklyn Butcher case. These fingerprints matched those of Louis Masgay, a Pennsylvania man who had been missing for two and a half years. Zugibe's frozen theory was correct. Police learned that an informant had seen a body fitting Louis's description hanging in a warehouse freezer that belonged to Richard Kuklinski, a suspected hit man. Richard was being watched by the FBI, and unknowingly told an undercover agent about the frozen body, helping to break the case.

"You think those guys are smart?" Kuklinski said, speaking of investigators. "Listen to me. They found this one guy, and when the autopsy was done, they said he was only dead two and a half weeks. But see, he wasn't. He'd been dead two and a half years."[1]

As it turned out, Louis had planned to meet with Kuklinski to buy pirated movies for resale in his general store. Instead, Kuklinski stole Louis's $95,000 and killed him. Kuklinski then staged the crime scene by freezing the body, which earned him the nickname "the Iceman." Kuklinski was sentenced to life in prison for six murders and claimed to have committed 250 in all.

No matter how diligently medical examiners work, some bodies found in clandestine graves are never identified and the cases are never solved. In 1989, an owner of the Good'nLoud Music store

Richard Kuklinski, known as "the Iceman," being led into trial for murder

near the University of Wisconsin was investigating a leak in the heating system when he found a human skull in the basement. Police and fire inspectors came on the scene and found an entire skeleton, shoved feetfirst down the chimney chute. It had lost all soft tissue.

The body was dressed in a sleeveless paisley dress, dark shag sweater, ankle socks, and women's shoes. And yet the forensic scientists working the case agreed that the skeleton belonged to a man, between twenty-two and twenty-seven years old. Investigators theorized that the victim was transgender and had been killed for this reason. (Transgender people are 28 percent more likely to suffer from violence.) However, the forensic scientists weren't even sure that a murder had occurred at all. The victim's only apparent injuries were fractured pubic bones, and that could have happened after death when the body was pushed down the narrow flue. In hopes of learning more, detectives made a clay model and computer-assisted sketch of the victim's face (as a man) and shared it with the public. But no one came forward who could identify the skeleton. Those who knew the victim might have moved on long ago, as college towns have a large transient population of students, or the victim could have been unrecognizable as a man. Whatever the case, no more was ever learned of the person's life—or death.

9
Dem Bones:
Forensic Anthropology Beginnings

When bodies are badly decomposed, or only the skeletons remain, forensic anthropologists may be called in. Forensic anthropology became an official branch of forensic science in the 1970s. Since then, it has been used to solve cases old and new.

A forensic anthropologist's first step is to determine whether the body is ancient (five hundred years or older), historic (fifty to five hundred years old), or contemporary (less than fifty years old). Next, the scientist decides whether the person died of natural causes or was murdered. When two German hikers found a corpse in the Italian Alps on September 19, 1991, the rescue team first assumed it was a hiker who had gotten lost and died of exposure. Though the body was well preserved by the snow, it soon became clear that neither assumption was true. Instead, the body was very old, and the person hadn't frozen to death. He was murdered.

Konrad Spindler, an Austrian professor of prehistory, determined the body to be at least 4,000 years old. Carbon-I4 analysis further indicated that it was 5,000 years old—placing his time of life at the end of the Stone Age. The man, nicknamed Ötzi for the Ötztal Alps where he was found, was between forty and fifty-three years old at his time of death. The years had been unkind. His growth had been stunted by childhood hunger. Campfires had blackened his lungs. His toes had been repeatedly frostbitten. His teeth were rotting, and he had gum disease. His body contained a large amount of arsenic, probably from working with copper. An analysis of his fingernails showed he had suffered several bouts of illness in his last six months—including intestinal worms and possibly Lyme disease. Today, some of these ailments would suggest a lack of resources and medical aid endured by only the poorest of the poor. But during the Stone Age, such hardships were common.

Re-creation of Ötzi, a five-thousand-year-old murder victim

In spite of his poor health, Ötzi must have had a hearty appetite. His stomach was so well preserved that scientists could tell his last meal was red deer and cereal. He'd also eaten, within a short time before his death, wild goat and bread baked in an open fire (as indicated by fragments of wheat and charcoal in his stomach). The iceman must have traveled widely, for archeobotanists found eighty species of mosses and liverworts in and on his body, and dozens of pollen grains. One was from the hop hornbeam tree, which grows in the valley below the Alps and blooms in the spring. Archeologists hypothesized that Ötzi's journey began in the valley and ended in the snowy Alps.

He could have frozen to death in a late snowstorm, but his injuries pointed to a different cause of death. Scientists found an arrowhead inside his left shoulder and an entry wound on his back. According to X-rays, the arrow must have pierced a blood vessel, causing Ötzi to bleed to death. He had been murdered.

Determining the cause of death in a 5,000-year-old cold—or rather, freezing—case was pretty good detective work. Was it possible to determine the murderer and motive, too? Archeologists theorized that Ötzi knew his attackers. The arrow shaft was missing from his shoulder wound, and someone had to have pulled it out. This would have covered up the identity of the killer, as arrows were unique to their owners. Also, the killer stole none of Ötzi's belongings, even though such items would have been hard to come by during the Stone Age. Again, possession of these would have linked the killer to the crime.

Like medical examiners working a contemporary case, archeologists also studied what Ötzi had on his person at the time of death. In some ways, he seemed prepared for his wilderness trek. He wore three layers of clothing, and shoes with bearskin soles, and carried a fire-starting kit. He also had a nice dagger, suggesting high social status. He had other weapons, too, but they were only half finished. The arrows were incomplete and his longbow unstrung. He seemed to have left on the fly. He had a partially healed hand wound—likely from a fight that had happened a day or so before his death—and a head injury, suggesting a fall while on the run, or an outright attack.

Based on this evidence, archeologists theorized that Ötzi was the leader of his tribe. When old age and sickness weakened him, other tribe members tried to take over. They fought with him in the village, and, fearing assassination, Ötzi fled. His enemies caught up to him and killed him. Archeologists will never know for sure if this is what happened. And no charges were ever filed, obviously.

The cause of death is not always so clear in ancient cases. Several bodies from the Iron Age (1200 BCE to 550 CE) have been found in bogs across Northwest Europe. Though thousands of years old, they are relatively well preserved by the lack of oxygen in the stagnant waters. They still have skin, hair, and, in some cases, the clothing they wore. Early researchers believed that people were buried in the bogs as punishment. A Roman historian wrote that Germanic peoples shaved the heads of disgraced sinners, killed them, and threw them in the bog instead of cremating them, which was the standard burial practice. When two bog bodies were found in Germany in 1952, one with long red hair that was shorn on one side, researchers theorized that they were secret lovers. They named the half-shaven one "Windeby Girl" and supposed that she had been shaven prior to being killed as a way of disgracing her.

Later, DNA testing revealed Windeby Girl to be a man. His bones indicated that he was sickly—and could easily have died of disease instead of a death sentence. Half his hair, which would have been dyed red by the sphangnum moss in the bog, might have been lost during excavation. The "lover" found nearby had lived three hundred years before Windeby "Girl." Likewise, many bog bodies have been examined for violent injuries—but whether these were part of brutal attacks or simply the result of the bodies' time in the bogs is unclear. While these bog bodies are a matter of great historical interest, they're not exactly parts of criminal investigations. But in one case, a bog body did lead to a murder being solved.

Bogs produce peat, which is cut out of the soil and used as fuel. In 1983, workers digging out peat in England found a human skull. Investigators determined it to belong to a female between the ages of thirty and fifty. Twenty-two years earlier, Malika Reyn-Bardt had gone missing, and police had long suspected her husband, Peter Reyn-Bardt. Faced with what he thought was his wife's skull, Peter confessed to the murder and was found guilty. But it turned out the skull was around 1,600 years old, giving Reyn-Bardt a pretty solid alibi—for that crime, anyway.

Forensic anthropology in historic cases (fifty to five hundred years old) can have contemporary implications. After the Russian royal family—the Romanovs—were massacred as part of a political uprising in 1918, there was speculation as to whether any of the children had escaped. One woman even claimed for several decades to be Anastasia Romanov.

During World War I, 1.7 million Russian soldiers were killed, and nearly 7.5 million wounded, captured, or ruled missing in action. The Russian economy was in shambles from funding the war. The people rioted, blaming Tsar Nicolas II for the disaster. He abdicated in 1917, and a provisional government took power. Months later, the radical Bolshevik Party, led by Vladimir Lenin, overthrew the provisional government, and Lenin became dictator. Though he ended Russia's involvement in the war in Europe, Lenin was faced with a civil war at home. The White Army, made up of Royal allies and other anti-Bolsheviks, fought to regain power. Meanwhile, the Romanovs were living under Bolshevik guard in a mansion in the Ural Mountains. The White Army was pushing toward this location, and there was hope of a rescue.

Portrait of the Romanov family

Then, on July 17, 1918, the Romanovs were awakened in the middle of the night and informed that they were being moved to another home because of the fighting nearby. The family—Tsar Nicholas II and Tsarina Alexandra Feodorovna; their daughters, Olga, Tatiana, Maria, and Anastasia; their son, Alexei; his doctor, Yevgeny Botkin (who treated Alexei for hemophilia); a cook, Ivan Kharitonov; a footman, Alexei Trupp; and a maid, Anna

Demidova—were moved to a room downstairs, where they were to await transportation. Jewels and other family treasures were hidden in pillows the family carried, and Anastasia's corset was lined with jewels as well.

Soon, the family learned their true fate. Bolshevik commander Yakov Yurovsky entered, accompanied by a death squad, and read a decree of execution. He shot Tsar Nicholas first. Then the firing squad, which had gotten drunk to numb themselves to the brutality, haphazardly opened fire. Anna hid behind the jewel-filled pillows but was discovered and killed. Anastasia's corset served as a bullet-proof vest of sorts, and she survived the first moments of the attack. Afterward, the bodies were stripped, the clothes burned, and the jewels sent to Moscow. The execution was supposed to be a state secret, so Yurovsky hid the bodies in an abandoned mineshaft, but he moved them when word got out of their location. To hide the identity of the victims, he doused them with hydrochloric acid and burned the bodies that he thought were the tsar and tsarina.

Eight days after the massacre, the Russian White Army conquered the Siberian town of Ekaterinburg and searched the mineshaft. They found evidence of the bodies having been there, including the tsarina's eyeglass case, but couldn't find the new graves. The location would remain a mystery for years to come, leading people to wonder if some of the Romanovs had survived.

In 1920, a woman was rescued from a Berlin canal after attempting suicide. She was confined to an asylum, where she told a fantastic story. She had survived a Russian firing squad and was found alive on a truck carrying the dead bodies. She was secreted away and had wound up in Berlin. She was Anastasia Romanov! In 1928, the woman traveled to America, purportedly for jaw surgery due to injuries from the massacre. She was greeted as a celebrity by some and dear friend by others. Gleb Botkin—the son of Dr. Botkin who had died in the massacre—had played with Anastasia as a child. He was overjoyed to see her again. But others were skeptical. A private investigator hired by the royal family said that "Anastasia" was really Franziska Schanzkowska, a Polish peasant who had vanished three days before the incident on the bridge and had a history of mental illness. But the woman known as Anna Anderson (a fake name she once gave at a hotel in lieu of Anastasia) stuck to her story until her death in 1984.

Anna Anderson, who claimed to be the youngest daughter of Tsar Nicholas

In the 1980s, Soviet Union leader Mikhail Gorbachev declassified documents from the Bolshevik regime, including the Yurovsky Note, which described the assassination. According to the note, Anastasia had evaded the rain of bullets for a time but was eventually killed during the attack. Evidence could be found in the forest, where Yurovsky had buried the bodies.

People were determined to see for themselves whether this was true. In 1992, an American team of forensic anthropologists excavated the Romanov grave to account for those killed in the attack. The team found nine skeletons instead of the expected eleven. They were able to match the skeletons to most of the victims. One female skeleton had extended ankle joints caused by crouching or kneeling. That belonged to the maid, Anna. Another skeleton lacked upper teeth—that was the doctor. A tall, large-boned skeleton belonged to the footman, who was over six feet tall. The tsar was identified by his jutting brow line and hips deformed from horseback riding. The tsarina's dental work matched another skeleton's. A skeleton with incomplete molars belonged to either Maria, who was nineteen, or Anastasia, seventeen. Tatiana, the tallest of the sisters, was matched to a skeleton of the correct height. Olga was known by her wide forehead. The cook, an adult male, was linked to a skeleton by the process of elimination. And that was all. Where were Alexei and either Maria or Anastasia? Could Anna Anderson have been telling the truth?

DNA from the bodies was tested against that of England's Prince Philip (husband of Queen Elizabeth II), whose grandmother was the tsarina's sister. It was a match. Anna had since passed away, but tissue samples had been saved. The DNA from these was tested against DNA from the bodies. They were not a match. Instead, her DNA matched the relatives in Poland that the private investigator had tracked down years ago. Still, the missing children—who would now be an elderly man and woman—*could* be elsewhere (though the likelihood of Alexei's having survived the attack was slim given his health problems).

Then, in 2007, a team searching for the lost bodies near the Romanov grave hit bone and dug deeper. They found skeletons badly damaged by acid and fire. The DNA matched the Romanov family. Alexei and his sister had been found, and the story brought to a close. It just wasn't the ending anybody wanted.

From these stories, it's not surprising that much can be learned from a contemporary skeleton. With just a skull, dental records can tell the identity of the victim. The pelvic bone and skull indicate whether the skeleton is male or female. Age can be determined by the number of bones in a body. Babies are born with 270 bones. Over time, these fuse together, until, at age twenty, an adult has 206 bones. Bones can even show whether a person was right- or left-handed, the bones having a higher density and often being slightly longer in the dominant arm. And marks on bones show the type of wound that was suffered.

In July 1982, blackberry pickers in Goochland County, Virginia, found human bones in a berry patch. The lower part of the body was missing, probably having been devoured by animals. Jeans and a red jersey were found nearby. Dr. J. Lawrence Angel, a curator at the Smithsonian and the FBI's consultant in forensic anthropology (nicknamed Sherlock Bones by the press) determined it to be that of an eighteen- to twenty-four-year-old. The skull and smoothness of the brow indicated she was female. She was around five feet tall and thin but broad shouldered. She had a large skull, strong chin, and thin, asymmetrical nose. Her left little finger had been injured— possibly from a defensive wound against a knife.

The next January, the body was linked to a missing woman from Arlington, Bilmaris Rivera. On May 24, 1980, she had left for work as a chemist on a marine base, but never made it. Her car was found on fire two days later, with no body inside. Dental records from her native Puerto Rico confirmed the match. However, the case went cold, and the bones were shipped to the woman's family for burial. Angel passed away.

Then in May 1991, the Goochland County commonwealth's attorney made an arrest and ordered the body exhumed. He asked

Angel's successor, Douglas Ubelaker, to examine the body. In particular, he sought information about the wounded finger. To everyone's disappointment the grave was waterlogged. The finger might have been be lost. But when the casket was opened, investigators found the finger protected in a bag, its contents labeled in Angel's handwriting. He had somehow known to preserve the finger with extra care.

As with the bog bodies, the forensic anthropologist couldn't be sure if the finger injury had happened before or after death. Her body had clearly been damaged while in the woods. Some bones were missing, and others had tooth marks, indicating that animals had fed on the carcass. However, the finger wound was unlike the others; it was clear-cut, as though sliced off, not chewed. Ubelaker did experiments to determine what could have caused such an injury. One possibility was that the finger had been injured when slammed in the door of Bilmaris's Pinto. Substituting chicken bones for the finger bone, he tested this theory. The cuts were similar on the chicken bones. The case never went to court. The damaged finger, and perhaps the possibility of its having been slammed in a car door, must have looked bad enough for the suspect to plead guilty. This shows that a body—no matter how poor the condition—is extremely helpful in an investigation. But the lack of a crime scene makes the puzzle hard to piece together. That's because so very much can be gleaned from the scene of the attack. For that reason, it's where criminal profilers do much of their work.

10
To Catch a Killer: Criminal Profilers

The FBI established its Behavioral Science Unit in the 1970s. It was dedicated to investigating high-profile or difficult-to-solve murders by studying how murderers think and behave—in other words, through criminal profiling. FBI profilers are perhaps best known for tracking down serial killers by looking for patterns at crime scenes. In fact, the term *serial killer* was coined by one of the FBI's early profilers, Robert Ressler. But by then, serial killers—and psychological profiling—had existed for nearly a century. Perhaps the most notorious serial killer was Jack the Ripper, mentioned in the introduction, and so named because his true identity was never known.

London in the late 1800s was the richest city in the world. But the wealth didn't flow into its East End neighborhoods. These were flooded instead with poor immigrants from Ireland and Europe, who joined the poor natives of England in the crowded tenements.

In such a cramped, deprived, and disease-ridden environment, alcoholism flourished, and with few options for employment, many women turned to prostitution. Fifteen hundred prostitutes worked in the Whitechapel neighborhood alone. Yet for all its ills, random murders were uncommon in Whitechapel. People killed people they knew, whether in rage or for some personal gain. That's how the Ripper case was investigated at first.

The body of Mary Ann "Polly" Nichols was found in a Whitechapel gateway at three forty-five a.m. on August 31, 1888, her throat cut and her body mutilated with a knife. The men who found the body summoned a police officer, but by the time he arrived, another policeman, Constable John Neil, had also made the discovery. The time of death was quickly determined. A police officer had walked past the gateway a half hour before, and so the killing must have occurred minutes earlier. A woman was sleeping in a room above the gateway but heard no scream. That meant the killer had probably taken Polly by surprise and killed her instantly, mutilating her quickly before fleeing the scene.

Such an escape would not have been difficult. London streets were lit by dim gas lamps. Even in the middle of the night, the streets of Whitechapel were well traveled by prostitutes, drinkers, and those walking to and from their factory night shifts, but the darkness and the black clothing worn at the time would have concealed the blood on the killer.

A doctor was called in to examine the body. He noted that the cuts on the body ran left to right, meaning the killer might have been left-handed. The weapon appeared to have been a dagger or sharp knife and wasn't left at the scene. Next, police worked to identify the victim. "Lambeth Workhouse" was stenciled on her petticoats, and a worker there was able to identify the body as Polly, who had since moved out. She had most recently lived in a lodging house and worked as a prostitute. Her new housemate, Ellen Holland, had last seen Polly at two thirty a.m. She'd said she was going out to find a customer so that she could pay her rent.

As in most murder cases, investigators questioned the people Polly knew. She had been married with five children but left them when the youngest was still a toddler. Her ex-husband said their marriage had broken up because of her drinking. Her father said it was because the husband had had an affair. Whatever the reason, the husband hadn't seen Polly in three years. The police suspected neither man in the murder.

Polly wasn't the first woman in Whitechapel to be violently killed that year. There had been two other prostitutes murdered—in April and August. Police investigated Jack Pizer, a man who was said to be blackmailing prostitutes and assaulting them. His alibi cleared. On closer look, the three murders were dissimilar. The first victim survived long enough to say there had been three assailants. The second victim was stabbed repeatedly, but not mutilated like Polly.

Whether or not these were early Ripper victims is still debated today. Either way, police knew all too soon that a single killer was targeting the neighborhood's prostitutes. The next victim, Annie Chapman, was found in a backyard on Hanbury Street at around six a.m. on September 8, 1888. The wounds were similar to Polly's, and like that murder, this attack had happened quickly. Annie had been seen talking to a man on the street just minutes earlier. A witness described him as "shabby-genteel," dark, in his forties, and wearing a deerstalker hat.[1] The doctor who examined the body suggested that based on the cuts, the killer might have had a background in medicine. Doctors and medical students were investigated.

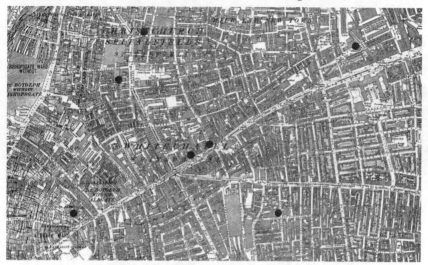

Map showing the locations of the Whitechapel murders

On September 25, 1888, the Central News Agency received a letter addressed "Dear Boss" and signed by "Jack the Ripper." In it, the killer promised to cut off the ear of his next victim. It was at first thought to be a hoax. But in the early morning hours of September 30, the bodies of Elizabeth Stride and Catherine Eddowes were found less than an hour apart in separate locations. Eddowes's ear was sliced from top to bottom. Her body was also mutilated, and a kidney removed.

A piece of her bloody apron was found near the body, and above it, written in chalk, were the words, "The Juwes are the men that Will not be Blamed for nothing."[2] Though a photograph could have been taken (they were taken of the bodies in the morgue), Metropolitan Police Commissioner Sir Charles Warren didn't want to wait for a photographer to arrive. He was concerned that with day-break near, people would see the words and be inflamed against the Jewish immigrants in the neighborhood. So he erased the writing. Afterward, the men who saw it disagreed on the misspelling. Was it "juwes" or "jewes" or "juews"? This could have been an important clue, as crimes have been solved by having a suspect write a message and checking the misspellings against each other. They also could have compared the handwriting side by side to the letters purport-edly written by Jack the Ripper—and there were more to come.

The Central News Agency received a letter on October I that said:

> *I wasn't codding dear old Boss when I gave you the tip. You'll hear about saucy Jacky's work tomorrow double event this time number one squealed a bit couldnt finish straight off. had no time to get ears for police. Thanks for keeping last letter back till I got to work again.*
> *Jack the Ripper[3]*

Again, detectives couldn't tell if it was a hoax. The killer had intimate details of the crime, but perhaps they had been gleaned from news accounts. A couple of weeks later, the chairman of the East End Vigilance Committee, George Lusk, received a gruesome package—half of a kidney—and a letter. It said:

> *From hell*
> *Mr. Lusk*
> *Sir*
> *I send you half the*
> *Kidne I took from one women*

prasarved it for you. tother piece
I fried and ate it was very nise. I
may send you the bloody knif that
took it out if you only wate a whil
longer
signed Catch me when
you can
Mishter Lusk[4]

The kidney was determined to be human and was similar to Catherine Eddowes's other kidney. It didn't contain the preserving chemicals used in hospital autopsies. But such chemicals weren't used in autopsies conducted by medical students. If the letter had been a hoax, that might have been the source. Of course, nowadays, a simple DNA test of the body and the kidney could answer this question. As it was, the authenticity of the letters and package were never known.

Police tried a new approach to catching the killer. They brought in bloodhounds and were prepared to set them on the killer's trail if another victim was found. This may have scared the killer off for a while, but by the time the dogs were needed, they were no longer at the disposal of Scotland Yard. One hound, Barnaby, had been ordered home when the owner learned the dog had been used to track a burglar. He feared that neighborhood criminals would poison the beloved pet to avoid being caught.

And so the killer would get away with murder again. On November 9, twenty-five-year-old Mary Jane Kelly was found dead not in the streets but in her room, the youngest victim of Jack the Ripper. Her wounds were similar to the other victims', but her body was even more badly mutilated. Investigators believed the killer had spent more time with the body because of the privacy of the room. Scotland Yard took crime scene photos of the murder scene—the first of their kind. Mary Jane's murder also led to one of the first criminal profiles.

Dr. Thomas Bond, police surgeon in the Westminster section of London, was called on to examine Mary's body and read police notes from the previous Ripper murders in order to determine how much "surgical skill and anatomical knowledge" the killer had.[5]

Bond provided that information and more. In regard to the question of knowledge, Bond said the killer had none. "In my opinion he does not even possess the technical knowledge of a butcher or horse slaughterer or any person accustomed to cut up dead animals."[6]

Bond further provided the following criminal profile of the killer: "The murderer must have been a man of physical strength and of great coolness and daring. There is no evidence that he had an accomplice. He must in my opinion be a man subject to periodical attacks of Homicidal and erotic mania. . . . The murderer in external appearance is quite likely to be a quiet inoffensive looking man probably middleaged and neatly and respectably dressed. I think he must be in the habit of wearing a cloak or overcoat or he could hardly have escaped notice in the streets if the blood on his hands or clothes were visible."[7] Bond added that the killer likely kept odd hours and had no regular job. If the killer had a family, they likely suspected him in the murders.

Unfortunately, the profile did not lead to an arrest. But Ripper may have stopped killing. Other murders followed, but though in some ways similar, they didn't bear the clear marks of the earlier

Ripper murders. Many detectives believed that Mary Jane Kelly was Ripper's last victim, and that afterward, he was killed or committed to an insane asylum by family members who sensed his true identity.

Police had several suspects; one top investigator, Sir Melville Macnaghten, assistant chief constable, narrowed the list down to three in an 1894 report:

- M. J. Druitt, a doctor whose family believed him to be the murderer. His body was found in the Thames in late 1888, the victim of suicide.
- Kosminski, a resident of Whitechapel who hated prostitutes and had homicidal tendencies. He was confined to an insane asylum in March 1889.
- Michael Ostrog, a Russian doctor who was in and out of prison and suffered from "mania." He was released from prison in March 1888 and confined again November 18.

Many books and articles have come out purporting to name the real Jack the Ripper. Some even suggest that Ripper moved to America or Australia and became a serial killer there. But the fact that so many "real" culprits have been named shows that the killer is a mystery to this day. It is still challenging to track down a stranger killer. With no personal connection to the victim, and no obvious motive, the trail runs dry. Or so the murderer hopes. In the 1970s, the FBI made a science of tracking down these elusive killers—and through their work, many were brought to justice.

On October 12, 1979, Francine Elveson was found murdered in New York City. She was beaten, mutilated, and bitten. The only evidence found was a hair classified as African American, which would turn out to be a false lead. A six-month manhunt by the New York Police Department turned up nothing.

The department knew that the FBI had recently formed the Behavioral Science Unit. Its psychological profilers were visiting prisons and interviewing serial criminals to learn how they thought and acted. Through these interviews, profilers learned things that every armchair detective knows today: that criminals keep evidence as souvenirs, for instance, and that crimes tend to be clustered around areas familiar to the killer. John Douglas from the Behavioral Science Unit was called in to help with the case.

John Douglas from the Behavioral Science Unit

Douglas made several observations based on what the Behavioral Science Unit had learned from past crimes. For instance, he knew that the more time a killer spent at a scene, the more comfortable he was in that location. Based on the amount of time the killer spent at this scene, Douglas theorized that he either lived nearby or knew the victim. Douglas also said that because Francine was strangled by her purse strap, the crime was likely committed impulsively, suggesting mental illness. Contrary to the hair evidence, Douglas thought the murderer was white, as this type of crime usually occurs within the killer's own racial group.

The criminal profile was of an unkempt, unemployed white male, age twenty-five to thirty-five, who had a history of mental illness and lived nearby. This led police to Carmine Calabro, who was white, thirty years old, unemployed, and had a connection to the building—his father lived there. He did have a history of mental illness, but therein lay a problem: he was institutionalized at the time of the murder. However, as the investigation showed, Carmine had left the mental institute, committed the murder, and then walked back. The hair that had misled investigators at the start had been transferred from a contaminated body bag.

This case built a reputation for the Behavioral Science Unit, so other police departments sought their help. The unit also drew the attention of novelist Thomas Harris, who was researching the novel series that would include *The Silence of the Lambs*. For that book, he wanted his protagonist to be a female FBI agent, but there were none working in the Behavioral Science Unit at the time. Instead, he interviewed an agent outside the unit, Dr. Patricia Kirby. She would be influential in the creation of the character Clarice Starling.

Anthony Hopkins and Jodie Foster in the film *The Silence of the Lambs*

Kirby actually hoped to become part of the Behavioral Science Unit someday. She believed that because the majority of serial killers were men, and their victims overwhelmingly women, it would make sense to have women profilers. Their strength would be twofold: When conducting victimology studies, women would be able to relate to the victim. And when talking to a criminal, she said, "a woman will listen more and not judge and that lack of judgment entices someone to be more forthcoming." Kirby went to work for the Behavioral Science Unit in 1984.[8]

In Harris's book, released in 1988, FBI agent Clarice Starling interviewed the psychotic criminal Hannibal Lecter to gain insight into another serial criminal she was tracking, Buffalo Bill. Inspired by the character, more women FBI agents applied to the Behavioral Science Unit. Mary Ellen O'Toole was one such agent. Though her father had been an FBI agent, she actually became interested in investigative work while working as a security guard at a department store. In that capacity, she witnessed a man stealing a piece of jewelry—by swallowing it. She then talked him into coming to a back room, where another worker searched his bag for merchandise. Inside was a butcher knife. At the time, police were searching for a serial killer in the area. O'Toole wondered if this could be the guy. It wasn't, but the excitement of the moment spurred O'Toole to join the FBI, where she would help put many serial killers away.

Mary Ellen O'Toole, FBI agent

In a documentary about *The Silence of the Lambs* and the FBI Behavioral Science Unit, O'Toole explained the advantage of being a woman when interrogating a suspect. She said that serial killers don't tend to have normal relationships with women but are fascinated by them. "No matter how violent their crimes against female victims, they still, for the most part, love to talk with women," she said.[9]

O'Toole played a key role in investigating the Green River murder case. DNA evidence had linked Gary Leon Ridgway to several women's bodies found near Washington State's Green River. They sought his confession for other killings in which there was no DNA evidence. Gary had an incentive to confess: if he did, prosecutors would not seek the death penalty. But he was a pathological liar and so would lead investigators on treks to find the bodies and then pretend he couldn't remember where they were. Investigators grew tired of this routine and called in O'Toole. By talking to him in a warm and friendly way, she led him to confess to the suspected murders—along with killings the police didn't even know about. He even drew O'Toole an accurate map of where the bodies could be found.

Investigators search for the remains of one of Gary Leon Ridgway's victims.

The Behavioral Science Unit is known for its work in catching serial criminals, but the unit actually helps law enforcement in other hard-to-crack cases as well. FBI profiler Gregg McCrary was called on to help in a strange and tragic case known as the Buddhist Temple Massacre. It took many twists and turns, but in the end, his initial reading of the crime scene proved to be correct.

On August 10, 1991, nine people were found murdered at the Wat Promkunaram Buddhist Temple outside Phoenix. Found by a temple workman, they lay in a circle—six monks: Pairuch Kanthong, Surichai Anuttaro, Boochuay Chaiyarach, Chalerm Chantapim, Siang Ginggaeo and Somsak Sopha; a monk in training, Matthew Miller; a nun, Foy Sripanpasert; and another temple worker, Chirasak Chirapong. It appeared that they had been kneeling in prayer. Because of the heinous nature of the crime and the interest both in America and Thailand (the birthplace of the monks and many of the temple worshipers), the FBI was called in to assist. McCrary hopped on a plane with a colleague.

Criminal profiling starts with an analysis of the crime scene. At the temple, signs pointed to there being two killers. For one thing, there were two different brands of cigarettes found at the scene, and there was evidence of two guns being fired. Though the word "Bloods" was carved on the wall, the crime scene didn't point to a gang killing. Fire extinguishers had been sprayed around the temple, nonsense that wouldn't have gone down in a killing for hire. Also, the bullets found came from a .22-caliber rifle, and a 20-gauge shotgun typically used for bird hunting. Gangsters aren't exactly known for weekend bird hunts; in the realm of shotguns, they tend to favor 12-gauge weapons.

Just as caliber is a measurement for rifles and handguns, gauge is a measurement used for shotguns. Like caliber, it indicates the diameter of the gun barrel, but inversely. The gauge describes the number of lead balls in a pound, with each ball being the maximum size to roll down the barrel of the shotgun. In a 20-gauge shotgun, twenty lead balls weigh one pound. In a 12-gauge shotgun, just twelve of the balls weigh a pound, meaning the balls must be bigger, and the barrel in which they fit larger. Thus, a 12-gauge shotgun has a larger barrel than a 20-gauge. In other words, the *larger* the caliber, the larger the gun barrel, but the *smaller* the gauge, the larger the gun barrel. (Note that the lead balls aren't actually used as bullets in shotguns. Instead, shells filled with pellets—or shot—are used as ammunition.)

Police remove bodies from the Wat Promkunaram Buddhist Temple, where six monks were killed.

For McCrary, the evidence pointed to three things: "disorganization, youth, and stupidity."[10] He suggested that the investigators focus on young suspects who lived in the neighborhood. His victimology work drew the same conclusion. The victims at the temple weren't involved in drug smuggling, as investigators had first thought, but lived truly religious lives. It was unlikely they were targets in a gang killing.

On September 10, the task force learned that two teenage boys, Rolando Caratachea Jr. and Johnathan Doody, had been stopped for suspicious activity on August 21, and a .22-caliber rifle had been found on the passenger side of the car. The rifle was confiscated on September 10 but wasn't put through to firearm analysis right away.

That's because on the same day, a man from a Tucson psychiatric hospital called police, identifying himself as Mike McGraw and saying he knew who committed the crime. He named four men: Mark Nunez, Leo Bruce, Dante Parker, and Victor Zarate. The four other men, along with McGraw himself, were arrested and subjected to hours of interrogation. All but Zarate confessed. He was released when videotapes confirmed his alibi.

Russell Kimball, homicide chief for the sheriff's office at the time, has since said the interrogations were mishandled. He said that officers who had never dealt with murders or major crimes were allowed to interview the suspects, and some of the officers fed the suspects information about the crime. The officers wouldn't take no for an answer.

"We hammered on those guys until we broke their will, it was as simple and as bad as that," he told the *Arizona Republic*. "After a while they were willing to say anything."[11]

McCrary didn't think any of the confessions added up. Why would these men drive from Tucson to Phoenix to kill a group of holy people in a remote Buddhist temple? Later, all four men recanted their confessions. McGraw also denied ever calling the police. He said someone had used his name while making the call. Confessions or no confessions, police still planned to try the men, who were now known as the Tucson Four. That is, until results from the teens' .22 rifle finally came in. It matched the casings found at the scene.

Rolando, Johnathan, and Johnathan's best friend, Alessandro Garcia (with whom Johnathan said he'd fired the rifle recreationally), were picked up for questioning. Rolando said he had lent the rifle to his friends, Johnathan and Alessandro. Investigators ruled out Rolando as a suspect but questioned the two other teens, using the same hard-core tactics they had used with the Tucson Four. Alessandro at first confessed to committing the murders with the four men. But it soon became clear to investigators that the Tucson Four had nothing to do with the murders. They were released, and three went on to sue Maricopa County for its handling of the case, all winning damages totaling in the millions.

That left Johnathan and Alessandro. Alessandro was on the hook for another murder. After the temple massacre, he had convinced a girlfriend to help him kill a woman at a campground. Another man, who had falsely confessed to that crime, was released. Alessandro testified against Johnathan in exchange for prosecutors not seeking the death penalty in his murder trials.

Alessandro told investigators that he and Johnathan had donned their high school ROTC uniforms and gone to the temple with the borrowed .22-caliber rifle, along with a 20-gauge shotgun from Alessandro's house. They had knocked on the door and, upon being let in, held the victims at gunpoint while robbing the temple. Then Johnathan shot each victim in the head with the .22, while Alessandro fired four rounds at the victims with the 20-gauge. Alessandro said they had killed the people in the temple because they were witnesses to the robbery.

Johnathan told a different story. He confessed to being at the temple but didn't confess to killing anyone. He didn't testify at the trial at all. Both teens were sentenced to more than 270 years prison. But the case didn't end there. Johnathan appealed his case in 2011, and his conviction was overturned. The appeals court ruled that Johnathan's confession was invalid because investigators failed to properly read him his Miranda rights. They told Johnathan he had the right to an attorney *only* if he had committed the crime. Of course, all suspects have the right to an attorney, guilty or not. Johnathan was retried, with his confession no longer admissible as evidence. Alessandro's testimony could still be considered. In January of 2014, a jury found Johnathan guilty. He had been seventeen at the time of the killings. He was now thirty-nine. Because of this case, Arizona has since changed the way it interrogates suspects.

Ironically, the Miranda rights are named after a case against the State of Arizona. Ernesto Miranda pled guilty in 1963 to rape, kidnapping, and robbery. He appealed his case, and the US Supreme Court ruled that his confession was inadmissible because police had failed to inform him of his right to an attorney and right to remain silent. Miranda was later retried and convicted. But the stated right to an attorney has helped innocent people avoid confessing to crimes they didn't commit.

Forensic science such as profiling has shed light on both true and false confessions. But it isn't perfect. In the 1990s, a new forensic science method—DNA profiling—was proven to be so reliable that it led to the exoneration of several convicted criminals and cast a shadow on the forensic evidence originally used against them. DNA evidence has been used to convict and exonerate, and it's now changing the way forensic science methods are tested and presented in court.

11

One in a Trillion:
The Dawn of DNA Evidence

Long before DNA was used to solve crimes, detectives were faced
with a much more basic task: determining whether blood came from
a human or an animal. Today, it may be odd for a person to have
animal blood on their clothing unless they've been hunting, cooking,
or performing first aid on a pet moments before. But in those days,
people owned few sets of clothing, washed them infrequently, and
butchered their own animals. In short, it was a bloodier time. So a
man who'd made sausage the week before might be accused of murder due to the stains on his clothing, even though he was innocent.
(Of course, the hog might have thought otherwise.)

In 1887, Sherlock Holmes fictionally invented a new test for
human blood. A real-life reliable test for human blood was developed soon after, though it now seems like a process straight out of
Mary Shelley's *Frankenstein*. A rabbit was injected with human blood

serum (the liquid in which red blood cells float). The rabbit blood was then sucked out with a syringe and allowed to clot in a test tube. The serum of the rabbit blood was separated out. The blood being tested was then added to the rabbit serum, and if the serum turned milky, the blood was human.

Around the same time, it was discovered that humans have different types of blood. Since at least the 1600s, doctors had tried to save the sick and wounded through blood transfusions. Whereas this worked for some patients, most would go into shock and die. Scientists discovered that human blood sometimes reacted to the blood of another human in the same way it reacted to animal blood: by clotting. It was clear that some people's blood was incompatible with others'. Austrian scientist Karl Landsteiner showed why. He dropped some of his own blood into test tubes with various other colleagues' blood. Some mixtures resulted in clumping, while others did not.

This test resulted in the discovery of the human blood types we still know today. Typing depends on the antigens and antibodies people have in their blood. An antigen is a protein present in red blood cells. An antibody is a protein in the blood plasma that reacts to certain antigens. Type A blood has A antigens and B antibodies. Type B blood has B antigens and A antibodies. When type A and type B blood mix, the antibodies and antigens react, and the blood clumps. Type AB blood has antigen A and B, but neither type of antibodies, and so doesn't clump when it mixes with either type of blood. That means if you have type AB blood, the rarest type, you can accept blood from any donor. This is known as being a universal recipient. Type O is the opposite of type AB blood. It has no antigens. A type O donor, known as a universal donor, can donate to those with type A, B, AB, or O blood, but can accept blood only from type O donors. (That's why, on TV shows, doctors call for type O blood for a patient who needs a fast transfusion but whose blood type is unknown.) However, these blood types are just a starting point. There are also blood types within the broad categories, and so blood transfusions are a little trickier than that.

In 1915 Dr. Leon Lattes of the Institute for Forensic Medicine in Turin wondered if blood type could be used to solve crimes. In one case, he was able to show that a suspect was innocent. Aldo Petrucci was a repeat offender found with blood on his coat after a murder. He claimed to know nothing of the crime and said the blood was from a nosebleed. Lattes took blood from the victim, blood from Petrucci's coat, and blood from the suspect. Petrucci's blood type, and the blood from the coat, were type O. The victim's blood was type A. That cleared Petrucci of the crime. A blood type match could also be used to draw out a confession. But in truth, the likelihood of having type A, B, AB, or O blood is 40 percent, 11 percent, 4 percent, and 45 percent, respectively, in America. So, with the exception of AB blood, the presence of a certain blood type doesn't narrow the pool much.

Later, it was learned that in about 80 percent of people, blood type is also expressed through bodily fluids, such as tears or saliva. These people are known as secretors. This was cutting-edge science in 1939, when an elderly man was found murdered in Bournemouth, on the south coast of England. Walter Dinivan was a wealthy man whose grandson and granddaughter lived with him. They went to a dance one night and returned to find their grandfather badly beaten. He was taken to the hospital and died soon after.

There was evidence of a robbery, and cigarettes and a curler were found on the scene. The grandchildren told the Dorset police that their grandfather would sometimes hire prostitutes, which might have explained the cigarettes and curler. Scotland Yard detective Leonard Burt was called in to assist with the case, and his instincts told him that the scene was staged. For instance, a cigarette lying on a couch cushion had to have been put out before it was casually dropped there (which it was made to look like). Otherwise, it would have burned the fabric. Furthermore, prostitutes questioned about the incident laughed at the old-fashioned curler; it was the kind elderly ladies used.

England had been late to establish a police laboratory—the first was created in 1934 in Nottingham. It came in useful with this case. Investigators had the saliva on the cigarettes tested for blood type, and as luck would have it, the smoker was a secretor with the rare AB type. A staged crime scene points to a suspect who knew the victim, and police began investigating Walter's friends. Burt interviewed Joseph Williams, who was over seventy years old, but figured him too old to have beaten the victim so badly. Burt's opinion changed when a prostitute told them that the usually broke Joseph had suddenly come into a lot of cash.

Police confronted Joseph, and he admitted to going to Walter for a loan but balked at the suggestion of murder. They tried a different tack. Burt told Joseph not to worry. He was no longer a suspect. Burt even bought Joseph a beer at the pub and offered him cigarettes. If you've watched even a few detective shows, you know that it was all a trick. Police had the cigarettes tested—and sure enough, Joseph had the rare type AB blood. His ex-wife was also tracked down, and she said that she used the same type of curler found on the scene. At the trial, however, the defense called the saliva evidence unreliable, and Joseph was acquitted. After the verdict, he admitted his guilt to his defense attorney, who shared the admission only after Joseph's death.

The case could be repeated in modern times, only with the saliva being tested for DNA rather than blood type. And in the early days of DNA, the jury might have balked at that evidence, too. But in fact, DNA testing, assuming the sample size is large enough, is considered the most reliable forensic evidence available. When it is present, DNA evidence can indicate almost without question that the suspect was at the crime scene.

The structure of DNA was discovered in 1953 by James Watson, Francis Crick, Rosalind Franklin, and Maurice Wilkins. It was a watershed event, revealing the very recipe for all life on earth. DNA basically functions like this: The human body contains trillions of cells, and each cell contains a person's entire genome (all of their DNA). DNA is shaped like a long, twisted ladder, or double helix. Each ladder rung has two letters—either A and T or G and C (the same two letters always pair up). These letters stand for the chemical compounds adenine, thymine, guanine, and cytosine. Along each side of the ladder, the letters make three-letter words. Several words together make a gene. The genes are instructions for building proteins—which in turn are the building blocks of the human body.

DNA's role in forensic science would not come until decades after its discovery. In the 1980s, Alec Jeffreys of the University of Leicester developed a blood test to determine a person's DNA profile and suggested that it could be used in criminal investigations. The test has changed through the years. Today, it works like this: All human genomes are 99.9 percent alike, which explains why all humans are remarkably similar to each other. But just as no two people are exactly alike, no two genomes are exactly alike. Looking at the same place on a genome, one person may have a sequence of letters, such as GCAAT, repeat five times, whereas in another person, they repeat fifteen times. The five-time repeat may occur in, say, one out of twenty people. A second section of the genome is also examined, and a certain variety of that sequence may also occur in one in twenty people. Together, the two sequences occur in one in four hundred people. Add a third sequence, and you have a set of sequences that occurs in one in 8,000 people. (That is just a hypothetical example to show how the sequences add up to be less and less common in the population.)

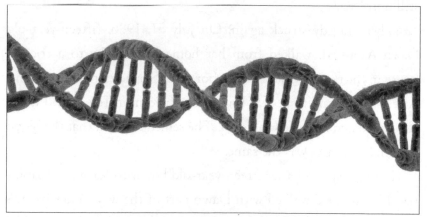

Structure of a DNA double helix

The US standard is to test thirteen sections of DNA, and together, those thirteen can only be found in one in a trillion people—more than the Earth's entire population. (The FBI recently recommended that even more sections of DNA be tested—twenty in all.) That's how investigators can link a DNA sample to just one suspect. Of course, no test is foolproof, but DNA testing is remarkably accurate and far more specific than a blood type test, which may only narrow down the pool to 45 percent of the entire population.

DNA evidence was first used to solve a murder in 1987, but the case began several years earlier. On November 21, 1983, fifteen-year-old Lynda Mann walked to a friend's home in the small village of Narborough, England, at around seven thirty p.m. Later that night, her parents learned that she had never come home. They searched the village but couldn't find Lynda. At seven twenty the next morning, a worker at the local psychiatric hospital made a heartbreaking discovery: Lynda, raped and strangled to death. Police suspected one of the inmates, but there was no evidence that any had left the hospital that night. After three years, the case was still unsolved.

Then tragedy struck again. On July 31, 1986, fifteen-year-old Dawn Ashworth walked from her home in Enderby to a friend's house in the nearby village of Narborough. She never returned home. After a long search, she was found in a field near Ten Pound Lane, also raped and strangled to death. The semen revealed that the blood type in both cases was the same.

Police suspected a seventeen-year-old boy with learning disabilities. He said he'd walked with Dawn part of the way to her friend's house. He didn't remember harming her but said perhaps he had gone crazy and done so. He later denied the possibility and never confessed to the first murder. Moreover, his mother said he had an alibi. His father had read about Dr. Alec Jeffreys and DNA testing and asked his son's attorney about it. The police agreed to test the teenage suspect's DNA, thinking that perhaps it would even link him to the first murder.

Jeffreys compared the DNA from the semen samples to the DNA in the young suspect's blood. The suspect's DNA was different from the semen samples, but the semen samples matched each other. The teenager was not the killer. But the two girls had been murdered by the same person. With the new forensic tool of DNA, investigators launched a revolutionary manhunt. They asked every adult male—4,500 in all—in the village and surrounding villages to volunteer a blood sample for testing. Those with type A blood would have their samples further tested for the DNA profile. DNA testing was new—and slow. After eight months, the testing had

found no matches. But while the high-tech testing occurred, a break in the case came from an old-fashioned source: gossip. A baker named Ian Kelly told coworkers at a pub

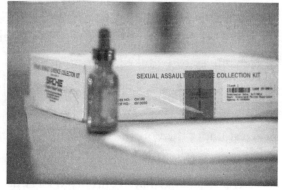

A sexual assault evidence collection kit, commonly called a rape kit

that, using a fake passport, he had given blood on behalf of another man. That man was Colin Pitchfork. Pitchfork had explained to the friend that he'd already given blood on behalf of another man and would get in trouble if he showed up again. One of the coworkers shared this information with the police, who began investigating

Pitchfork. His DNA was a match, and he confessed to both murders. He received two life sentences but was to be eligible for parole. In April 2016, Pitchfork was denied parole but recommended for a move to a lower-security prison.

The use of DNA evidence spread to America, and in 1994, federal law led to the creation of a national database for DNA—the FBI's Combined DNA Index System (CODIS). When bodily fluid, such as semen collected as part of a rape kit, is left at a crime scene, it is tested for DNA type. That DNA profile is entered into CODIS. CODIS also contains DNA profiles from people who have been convicted of or arrested for serious crimes. That varies from state to state. The federal government and twenty-eight states allow the DNA testing of a suspect *arrested* for a serious crime. The other twenty-two states take samples only after a person is *convicted* of a crime. That's a big difference, as a suspect is presumed innocent, while a convict is not. But the US Supreme Court recently upheld a state law allowing DNA samples to be taken after an arrest for a serious crime—not just after a conviction. The Court ruled that, like fingerprinting and photographing, a cheek swab for DNA testing is a reasonable part of an arrest under the Fourth Amendment, the right Americans have to not be searched or have their property searched without reason (evidence that they may have committed a crime). Legal experts believe that the Supreme Court ruling may lead other states to collect DNA samples during arrests.

Investigators are automatically notified by CODIS when DNA in the database matches DNA from a crime scene. So DNA taken from a suspect in a new case may lead to an old case being solved. In the case that led to the Supreme Court ruling, Alonzo King Jr. of Maryland was arrested in 2009 on an assault charge. A DNA sample was taken, which matched a DNA sample from a 2003 unsolved rape case. He was convicted of that crime. He argued that his right to privacy was violated when his DNA sample was taken before he was convicted of a crime. The Supreme Court's ruling, of course, said that it wasn't. (If a person is exonerated of a crime, they can have their DNA removed from the database, though it is a difficult process.)

When DNA testing first became available, it broke open a lot of cold cases. Chris Harvey became the director of cold case homicide investigations for Fulton County, Georgia, in 2005, after a federal grant allowed the county to revisit murder cases involving sexual assaults. Rape kits including semen samples were still on file for these cases. The samples had been taken to determine blood type, which could rule out suspects. Investigators didn't know at the time that these samples would one day do much more. Now Harvey's team could test for DNA and match that to people in the prison system (whose DNA samples had been taken due to their convictions). The results of DNA testing on the semen samples fell into four categories: no DNA profile was available (because the DNA had deteriorated over time), the profile was partial, the profile was complete, or the profile was complete and there was a CODIS match. The last category was the best-case scenario.

Investigators would then visit the suspect—who was often still in prison for the other offense—and ask in as many ways possible whether he knew the victim. If he denied it, that was all the better for investigators, as the suspect then had no explanation for his DNA being found at the scene. Harvey described the moment in which the suspect was told of the DNA match: "You'd go into the prison and they'd have no idea why you were there. And you'd watch their face change. They're thinking, 'Holy crap. I thought I'd gotten away with that.' It was like someone reaching out from the grave."[1]

If there was a full profile, but no CODIS match, the investigators would revisit each leading suspect and ask for a DNA sample. If the suspect refused, investigators could either seek a search warrant or go into stealth mode, following a suspect and obtaining a glass from which he drank or a cigarette that he smoked. In one case, they followed a suspect to a restaurant and asked the waitress for his glass. They found not one but three types of DNA on the glass. None matched the sample from the crime scene.

Even though the new convictions couldn't bring back the victims, the families were grateful for any resolutions. Although, as Harvey pointed out, in many murder cases the victim had no family. He or she lived a lonely life, and often a dangerous one involving drugs and prostitution. He said that resolving those cases was important to the detectives for that very reason. "Nobody cared about this person," he said. "Somebody had to stand up and be *for* this person."[2]

CODIS now contains 10.1 million DNA profiles from convicted criminals and 1.3 million more from arrestees. In 2013 alone 200,300 DNA matches were obtained through CODIS, which helped in 192,400 investigations nationwide. Just as DNA evidence has brought justice for victims, it has given those convicted a chance to prove their innocence. Many, including Johnnie Lee Savory, were just teenagers when they were sent to prison.

At age fourteen, Johnnie was accused of killing nineteen-year-old Connie Cooper and her fourteen-year-old brother, James Robinson. The two were found stabbed to death in their Peoria, Illinois, home on January 18, 1977. At first, the police thought Connie might have been raped, and that she and James were murdered so that they wouldn't identify her attacker. She was found with her nightgown pulled up above her waist, her underwear torn, and blood on the bed. A rape kit tested positive for semen. A week after the murders, however, the police dropped this theory and focused their investigation on James's friend Johnnie, with the motive instead being anger that erupted during a karate match with James.

Johnnie had had a tough life. His mother died when he was a baby, and he was being raised by his father. The police visited Johnnie at the end of one school day, and brought him to the police station, where the interrogation lasted until ten p.m. The next day, the interview ran from ten thirty a.m. to eight p.m. At first, Johnnie told police that he had visited James the day before the murders. The teen eventually confessed, but later recanted the confession.

Nevertheless, the trial centered on Johnnie's confession. But the evidence didn't match up. Hairs found in the two victims' hands were not similar to Johnnie's. Pants found in his home had type A blood type—Connie's blood type—but they were several sizes too large for Johnnie. His father, YT Savory, testified that the pants belonged to him, and that he had cut his leg a few weeks before. YT also had type A blood (along with 40 percent of the US population), and hospital records corroborated his injury. A pocketknife with a bloodstain was found in a pants pocket, but YT said he had used the blade to remove his stitches. Johnnie was convicted. But on appeal, a judge ruled that police had coerced his confession. A new trial was ordered.

At first, the state's attorney planned to drop the case. There simply wasn't enough evidence to convict Johnnie without the confession.

But soon, three new witnesses came forward—Frank, Tina, and Ella Ivy. The siblings had been interviewed by the police prior to the first trial but hadn't testified. At the time, they'd said that Johnnie had only told them that he knew that James and Connie had been murdered—not that he had done it. Now, the siblings said that Johnnie had also confessed to stabbing the two victims. (The Ivy siblings would later recant their testimonies.)

Prosecutors also focused on what Johnnie had told the police prior to his confession. He had said that on January 17, he'd been playing karate with James. They'd moved the TV to the floor so that it wouldn't get kicked over, and they'd cooked corn and hot dogs. But the police believed all that actually occurred on January 18, the day of the murders. The victim's mother said that on the morning of the eighteenth, she had cooked corn and hot dogs and left the food on the stove. When she came home and found the bodies, the television was on the floor and the kitchen in disarray. Police said that Johnnie's description of the home from January 17 was in fact a description of the crime scene. They theorized that during the karate match, he had flown into a rage. Of course, it's possible that in the process of eliciting the confession, police had provided Johnnie with information about the crime scene, and he was repeating details he had been told. Nevertheless, Johnnie was convicted again.

Then, in 1998, Johnnie was given new hope. Illinois passed a law allowing prisoners to have physical evidence from their cases tested, if the test hadn't been available at the time of their trials. Johnnie asked to test the pants and the victims' fingernail scrapings for DNA. The motion was denied. The Illinois Supreme Court ruled that YT

Savory had already testified that the blood on the pants was his. The court didn't mention the fingernail scrapings. The court also said that blood evidence on the pants alone wouldn't clear Johnnie of the crime. The testimony of the Ivys and Johnnie's own interview weighed too heavily on the case.

Johnnie continued to fight for the right to test DNA evidence gathered during the investigation. He was released from prison on parole in 2006, after serving almost thirty years. But he still wanted a third trial to prove his innocence. Northwestern University School of Law's Center on Wrongful Convictions of Youth took up Johnnie's case, and in 2013, a Peoria County circuit judge allowed testing of DNA evidence.

Johnnie's team tested the bloody pants, the knife found in the pants, fingernail clippings from Connie and James, semen from the rape kit, and a bloody light-switch plate from the crime scene. Unfortunately, the DNA in much of the evidence had decayed. Also, the hair evidence had been lost while in the state's custody. However, blood left on the light switch at the crime scene still retained its DNA. That was important because the prosecution had argued that James's blood had been transferred to the light-switch plate from the murderer's bloody hands. James's DNA was found in the blood, but so was a second DNA profile, matching neither of the victims, nor family members living in the home. Most importantly, it didn't match Johnnie's DNA. Johnnie's attorney, Joshua Tepfer, said, "It is the killer's DNA—and these results prove that the killer is not Johnnie Lee Savory." The semen from the rape kit also did not match Johnnie's DNA. Based on this evidence, Johnnie Lee Savory was pardoned by the governor of Illinois on January 12, 2015. Now a middle-aged man, he was still seeking a new trial to prove his child-hood innocence.

To date, DNA evidence has proven 329 wrongful convictions in America. At the same time, 141 real culprits were identified, who had together committed 145 additional crimes while out on the streets. DNA evidence may seem like a magic wand that erases past mistakes. But in fact, it is available in only a small percent-age of cases. Even when it is, it can be difficult for a defendant to gain access to that evidence. All fifty states have statutes allowing prison inmates access to DNA evidence from their cases. But there are hurdles. If a defendant confessed—or even pled guilty as part of a plea bargain—he or she is denied access to DNA evidence. Sometimes, the DNA evidence from the case wasn't adequately preserved. The Innocence Project is an organization that helps those convicted of crimes prove their innocence, often through DNA evidence. It recommends that the courts allow access to DNA testing in any case in which the evidence can establish inno-cence. It also recommends that DNA from past crime scenes be run through CODIS so that another culprit can potentially be found.

The Innocence Project is also examining how wrongful convic-tions occur in the first place. In many cases, human error, or just plain treachery, led to a wrongful conviction. In a study of 325 wrongful conviction cases, 235 involved the misidentification of a suspect by an eyewitness. In 88 cases, the suspect had made a false confession—often because of police coercion. In 48 cases, incor-rect or untrue information had been shared by police informants. Forensic science would seem to be an antidote for these mistakes and misdeeds. But in fact, bad forensic science was to blame in 154 of the cases studied.

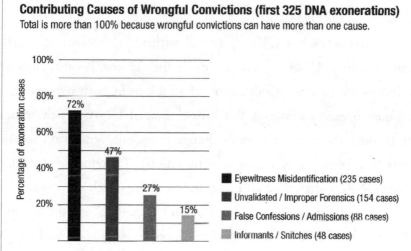

Contributing Causes of Wrongful Convictions (first 325 DNA exonerations)
Total is more than 100% because wrongful convictions can have more than one cause.

Innocence Project graph showing causes for wrongful convictions

In some instances, the forensic science was sound but its significance overstated. For instance, if type A blood was found at the scene, that may have ruled out a suspect with type B blood, but it certainly didn't implicate a suspect with type A blood—40 percent of the US population shares that blood type. If an expert said that the blood evidence meant that the suspect was at the crime scene, then he or she was misleading the jury.

The same is true of hair evidence. In the 1909 murder of Germaine Bichon in France, a thick, long blond hair found at the crime scene led to a confession. In truth, the hair could have come from any number of women, and indeed, the long interrogation could have brought about a false confession. Today, experts use DNA testing in conjunction with microscopic analysis of hair. Nuclear DNA, the type typically used to match crime scene evidence to a suspect, is usually present only if the hair root is attached, and even then just some of the time. When that fails, the hair can still be tested for mitochondrial DNA.

Whereas nuclear DNA is found within the nucleus of a cell, mitochondrial DNA is located outside the nucleus. Because nuclear DNA is the random combination of DNA from both parents, it is unique to each individual. But mitochondrial DNA, which comes from only the mother, doesn't change from one generation to the next (except in the rare case of a mutation). Therefore, mitochondrial DNA is shared by all maternal relatives, which may include a mother and child, siblings, cousins whose mothers are sisters, and even second and third cousins whose mothers were cousins through their mothers. And it includes male siblings and cousins, who share mitochondrial DNA but do not pass it on to their children. As you can see, several people can have the same mitochondrial DNA. But this type of testing does narrow down the pool of suspects to a single family. (It would not, however, link the sample to a convict in the CODIS system, which gathers mitochondrial DNA samples only in missing persons cases.)

Testing hair for mitochondrial DNA became routine at the FBI in 2000. Before then, many experts relied on microscopic analysis of hair alone and then gave misleading testimony about how specific such analysis could be. A study by the US Department of Justice, the FBI, the Innocence Project, and the National Association of Criminal Defense Lawyers found that in 95 percent of the 268 criminal trials reviewed, FBI hair analysts overstated the extent to which hairs could scientifically be matched. In thirty-two of those cases, the defendants were sentenced to death. Twelve hundred more cases involving hair analysis are currently under review. In some cases, there was other evidence against the defendant. However, all the defendants in those cases are being notified so that they can appeal their conviction if appropriate.

The FBI has acknowledged its errors and cooperated with the review of its hair analysis testimony. The Bureau now uses microscopic hair analysis in conjunction with DNA testing, and has written standards for its hair experts to explain results in court without overstating the science. It is creating similar standards for nineteen other areas of forensic science. It's a start. But legal experts say the courts should also be giving convicts recourse against bad forensic science. Currently, only two states—California and Texas—allow those convicted of a crime to appeal a case in which forensic testimony is recanted or proven invalid by scientific advances.

Not all evidence has to be scientific, of course. Laundry marks used to solve murder cases in the early twentieth century simply linked types of marks to laundries and their customer lists. Nothing too scientific about that. But when evidence is *presented* as being scientific, then it should have a scientific basis. Before DNA testing was used in murder investigations, it was vigorously tested by scientists. The results of the tests were published in peer-reviewed journals, meaning that fellow scientists had to agree that the tests were valid and the results clear. Other forensic science techniques have not been subjected to the same scrutiny. A prime example of that is bite mark analysis. In several cases, bite mark analysis helped to convict suspects who were later exonerated by DNA testing of the saliva found around the bite mark.

Roy Brown, exonerated for the murder of Sabina Kulakowski

One such suspect was Roy Brown, who became embroiled in a murder investigation that he himself would later solve. On May 23, 1991, firefighters were called to the scene of a raging fire consuming an Auburn, New York, farmhouse. Near the fire, they found the body of Sabina Kulakowski. She had been beaten, strangled, stabbed to death, and bitten. At first, the police investigated a man named Barry Bench. Sabina had dated his brother and still lived in the Bench family farmhouse. Barry had been to a bar the night of the murder. He had left the bar at twelve thirty a.m., and didn't arrive home until one thirty or one forty-five a.m. When he was called to the scene of the fire the next day, he was seen walking near where the body of Sabina was later found. He told others he was "trying to find evidence or find Sabina."[4] Barry's girlfriend told a friend she was "quite concerned when she found out that the body was found right where Barry was looking."[5] In spite of this strange fact, police soon turned their attention to Roy Brown.

A year before the murder, Roy's daughter had been removed from his home and placed in a residential care facility by the Cayuga County Department of Social Services. Afterward, Roy had made threatening phone calls to the department director, for which he had served jail time. He'd recently been released. Sabina was a social worker for the department. However, she hadn't handled Roy's daughter's case, and there was no evidence that the two had ever met. Roy was put on trial, and an expert witness testified that the bite marks found on the body were consistent with Roy's teeth. A defense expert countered the claim, saying that only one bite mark was complete enough to be analyzed, and that it showed two more upper teeth than Roy had. But the jury believed the prosecutor's expert and found Roy guilty. He would later say, "I can still remember looking at the jury in my trial when they heard the scientist testify. That's when I knew it was all over and I was going to prison, probably for the rest of my life."[6]

Roy did go to prison for a long time, but it wasn't all over for him. He was determined to prove his innocence. First, he sought DNA testing on saliva found at the crime scene. But he was told that the saliva had been used up during earlier testing. So Roy started playing detective. His copy of the trial records had been destroyed in a fire at his stepfather's house. From his prison cell, he wrote to the sheriff's department requesting a new copy. Under the state's Freedom of Information Law, the department was required to give this to Roy. The copy included four statements that Roy and his attorney say they had never seen before. All pointed to Barry Bench as a suspect.

Roy then wrote to the courts, saying that important statements had been withheld from him, in violation of state law. For instance, Barry said he'd driven directly home from the bar, but that meant he would have passed the farmhouse. By that time, it would have been in flames. Surely he would have done something about that. The court denied Roy's request for a new trial, saying that even if he hadn't been provided the Barry Bench documents, the information was not important enough to overturn the conviction.

Roy then went straight to the source. He sent a letter to Barry, saying that a DNA test would prove his guilt. He wrote, "Judges can be fooled and juries make mistakes, [but] when it comes to DNA testing there's no mistakes. DNA is GOD's creation and GOD makes no mistakes."[7] Five days after the letter was sent, Barry jumped in front of an Amtrak passenger train, killing himself. In 2005, the Innocence Project took up the case and discovered that saliva from Sabina's shirt was still available for testing. It did not match Roy's DNA. Project attorneys tracked down Barry's daughter. She gave a sample of her DNA, and half of it matched the crime scene saliva—typical for a parent-child DNA comparison. After fifteen years in prison, Roy was exonerated in 2007.

This is not just one man's tragedy. According to the Innocence Project, twenty-four others were falsely convicted based on bite mark analysis and later exonerated by DNA testing. Bite mark analysis has a rather sketchy history. During the Salem Witch Trials, Reverend George Burroughs was arrested for witchcraft based on bite marks

Engraving of a Salem witch trial

he'd supposedly left on girls. (According to the prosecutor's theory, the reverend had bitten the girls in order to turn them into witches.) The prosecutor looked into Burroughs's mouth and compared his teeth to marks found on the girls. Based on this evidence, Burroughs was hanged. Twenty years later, he was declared innocent—along with so many victims of the witch trials.

Such flimflam evidence could be expected of the Salem Witch Trials, where testimony about a woman seen shapeshifting into a cat was also allowed. But the same type of evidence was allowed three hundred years later, when Walter Edgar Marx was convicted of the California killing of a woman based on bite mark analysis. An appeals court upheld the 1974 conviction, saying that even though there was no scientific research to support bite mark analysis, the judge in the case had seen the bite mark comparison, and it looked good to him. This decision caused bite mark analysis to be allowed in other trials, only to be shown to be faulty later. In one case, an expert witness testified that the suspect's teeth matched a bite mark in a bologna sandwich found at the crime scene. The suspect was convicted, but an appeals court overturned the decision when the defense learned that the other half of the bologna sandwich was found in the victim's stomach during the autopsy, making it likely that the bite mark belonged to the victim. It's easy to single out bite mark analysis as unsound science, but other methods described in this book have also been questioned, including fingerprint and blood pattern analysis. Could some of the convictions described in this book have been wrongful due to faulty evidence? It's possible (and in the Cora Crippen murder, probable).

But that's not to say that older forensic science techniques should be thrown out the window. For one thing, they're needed to solve cases. Shows like *CSI* have led some people to believe that DNA evidence can crack any case. Legal experts call this the *CSI* effect. Jurors are reluctant to convict in cases where no DNA evidence is available, even when there is other solid evidence to go on. But in truth, slam-dunk DNA evidence is rarely left behind at crime scenes. Think about it: criminals may shed the blood of others, but how often do they shed their own blood, or, except in cases of rape, other bodily fluids?

That said, small samples of DNA—known as touch DNA—are often left behind when a suspect touches something. For the past ten years or so, investigators have gathered not only bodily fluids and hairs for DNA testing, but also the microscopic skin cells shed by suspects. Today's DNA tests are so sensitive that they can create a genetic profile from the skin cells found in a single fingerprint. However, this type of evidence is controversial. A test that can analyze such a small amount of DNA can also pick up DNA from someone who was never even at the crime scene. Say I shake hands with an old friend. That friend then goes and robs a bank. My skin cells, lingering on her hand, could be transferred to the bank safe.

University of Indianopolis scientists studied the likelihood of this scenario in 2015. Forensic scientist Cynthia M. Cale and her team had several pairs of people shake hands. Then each of them handled a clean knife. In 85 percent of the cases, DNA from the person who merely shook hands with the knife handler was found on the knife, and one-fifth of the time, the handshaker's DNA appeared to be the primary or only DNA sample found on the knife.

This phenomenon has had real-world implications. In 2013, a California man, Lukis Anderson, was arrested and held for several months when his DNA was found in the fingernail scrapings of a murder victim. But Lukis had a solid alibi: he was in the hospital being treated for intoxication at the time of the murder. As it turned out, the paramedics who transported Lukis to the hospital later responded to the murder scene and inadvertently transferred Lukis's DNA to the victim. That case, and the University of Indianapolis study, show that even cutting-edge science like touch DNA has its limits.

Old-fashioned as they may seem, footprints, fingerprints, hairs, and other physical evidence are still important to solving cases. The dawn of DNA hasn't changed that. But exonerations based on solid DNA evidence have shown that forensic science methods need to be tested, and that the scientific limits of each discipline need to be stated clearly. In 2009, the National Academy of Sciences released a report recommending that Congress create an independent board to establish standards for forensic evidence and techniques. The Department of Justice and the National Institute of Standards & Technology have since created the National Commission on Forensic Science, which will create uniform standards for forensic science. Their aim is to ensure that forensic science produces reliable evidence from scientifically rigorous methods.

The US attorney general will decide whether federal and federally funded labs will follow the recommendations. States will decide the extent to which they will follow the recommendations. The standards will also be a useful tool for attorneys on both sides of cases. Prosecutors and defense attorneys alike will be able to criticize expert witnesses whose forensic science doesn't meet the standards.

Now is an exciting time in forensic science. Investigators are using more and better techniques to bring about justice for victims, their families, those wrongfully accused, and communities shaken by violence. Today's forensic science is built on the work of the past. Imperfect as it may have been, it moved crime solving from darkness into light, where it is harder for criminals to hide—and for the falsely accused to be forgotten.

Glossary

accused   a person formally charged with a crime

acquittal   a court decision to declare a defendant not guilty

alibi   proof that a suspect couldn't have committed a crime due to having been seen in a different location

anarchist   a person who supports the end of government rule

appeal   a formal argument asking a higher court to reverse a decision made by a lower court

arsenic   a poisonous element

autopsy   the examination of a body to determine the cause of death

AWOL   an acronym for "absent without official leave"; fleeing when there is a legal obligation to stay

ballistics   the science of how a bullet travels through the gun barrel, air, and target

Bertillonage   a historical system of identifying criminals by taking various body measurements; also called the Bertillon system

bite mark analysis the now largely debunked science of matching a bite mark to a suspect's teeth

blood type the classification of a person's blood, based on the types of antigens and antibodies present

boardinghouse a residence in which bedrooms are rented and living spaces are shared among renters

bootlegger during Prohibition, a person who mass-produced, transported, distributed, or sold alcohol

cadaver a dead body, usually being held for the purpose of autopsy

caliber the diameter (in hundredths of an inch) of a gun barrel

carbon monoxide a poisonous gas released when fuels such as gas, charcoal, or wood are burned in an unventilated area

clandestine grave a site where a dead body is hidden

CODIS the acronym for "Combined DNA Index System," the FBI's database of suspects' DNA

cold case an unsolved investigation that is put on hold until new leads or resources are available

coroner an official who investigates violent or unexplained deaths

corpse a dead body

corpus delicti literally, "body of the crime"; in legal terms, proof that a crime occurred

criminal profiling an investigation strategy in which a criminal's thought and behavior patterns are considered

crowner the British official charged with seizing the property of criminals for the crown

cyanide a plant-based poison

defendant in a criminal case, the person charged with the crime

defensive wound an injury suffered in the course of fighting an attacker

DNA deoxyribonucleic acid, a collection of chemical compounds (adenine, thymine, guanine, and cytosine) that, together, form instructions for an organism to build and operate itself

DNA testing a process by which various sequences of adenine, thymine, guanine, and cytosine are compiled, creating a DNA profile that can be compared to other profiles

evidence items or information that tell how a crime occurred

exhume to remove a body from its grave

expert witness a person who draws on knowledge of a particular subject to testify at a trial

false confession a suspect's admission of a crime he or she did not commit

FBI Federal Bureau of Investigation, the law enforcement agency in America that handles federal crimes and domestic security issues

fingernail scrapings material found under a victim's or suspect's fingernails

forensic anthropologist a scientist who studies the skeletal remains of victims as part of criminal investigations

forensic entomologist a scientist who studies insect evidence in criminal investigations

forensic pathologist a scientist who studies the corpses of victims to gather evidence for criminal investigations

forensic science the use of science to solve crimes

gauge in ballistics, a measurement that inversely relates to the barrel size of a shotgun

hit man a person hired to kill someone

homicide   the killing of one person by another person

hung jury   a jury that is unable to reach a consensus after deliberation

jury   a group of laypeople in a legal case who weigh evidence and make a decision

luminol   a chemical used to detect the presence of blood

medical examiner   a medically trained official who investigates violent or unexplained deaths

Miranda rights   the warning police officers are required to give a person taken into custody, basically stating that a suspect has the right to remain silent and be represented by an attorney

mistrial   a court trial that ends before a verdict is reached, due to unusual circumstances or a hung jury

mitochondrial DNA   DNA inherited from the mother and located outside the cell nucleus

morgue   a place where bodies are stored and, in some cases, autopsied

motive   a person's reason for committing a crime

no-body case   a murder case in which the victim's body is not found

philter   potion

postmortem   after death

Prohibition   the Constitutional amendment, enacted in 1920 and repealed in 1933, forbidding the mass production, transportation, and distribution of alcohol

prosecutor   an attorney who represents the community in seeking the conviction of a defendant in a criminal case; the prosecutor's office may be that of the district attorney, the state's attorney, or the attorney general—different states and communities use varying terminology

racketeering   making money through illegal business activities

rape kit   a collection of materials used to gather evidence from a victim in a sexual assault crime

recant   to formally withdraw a statement or belief

remand   in a court case, to send a case to a lower court for further action

rifling   the spiral grooves inside the barrel of a firearm

Scotland Yard   a metonym for the headquarters of the London Metro Police, and the police force itself

secretor   a person whose blood type is expressed in other bodily fluids

serial killer   as defined by the FBI, one who murders two or more people, with the incidents happening at separate times

serology   the study of blood

staging   the alteration of a crime scene in order to confuse investigators

stay of execution   an official order to delay the death penalty of a prisoner

strychnine   a plant-derived poison

suspect   a person believed to be guilty of a crime

Tommy gun   a Thompson submachine gun

touch DNA   a small sample of DNA, often left behind when a suspect touches something

tour man   in the past, the term used to describe the medical examiner who visited the crime scene

toxicology   the study of the effects of drugs and poisons on a body

trace evidence   small amounts of material transferred from the perpetrator to the crime scene, or vice versa, in the process of a crime

ultimate issue   the question upon which a verdict hinges

verdict   a decision by a judge or jury in a court case

victim   a person hurt in a crime, accident, or other action

victimology   the study of factors that put a crime victim at risk

witness   a person who testifies during a trial about first-hand or expert knowledge

workhouse   in UK history, a building in which the poor worked and lived

Notes

Abbreviated citations have been used for some sources. Full information for these sources can be found in the Bibliography beginning on page 235.

Chapter I: A Whiff of Garlic: The First Poison Tests

1. Heinzelman and Wiseman, eds., *Representing Women*, 317.
2. Ibid.
3. Heslop, *Murderous Women*, 61.
4. Ibid., 60.
5. Livingston, *Arsenic and Clam Chowder: Murder in Gilded Age New York*, 5.
6. Ibid., 6.
7. Ibid., 7.
8. Fowler, *Deaths on Pleasant Street*, 39.
9. "More Swopes Died by Being Poisoned," *Oregonian* (Portland,

OR), February 13, 1910, http://oregonnews.uoregon.edu/lccn/sn83045782/1910-02-13/ed-1/seq-6/.

10. "Swope Poison Case Must Be Retried," *New York Times*, April 12, 1911, http://query.nytimes.com/mem/archive-free/pdf?res=9403EFDE1031E233A25751C1A9629C946096D6CF.

11. Ibid.

12. Benedetta Faedi Duramy, "Women and Poisons in 17th Century France," *Chicago-Kent Law Review* 87:2 (April 2012): 353, http://scholarship.kentlaw.iit.edu/cgi/viewcontent.cgi?article=3837&context=cklawreview.

Chapter 2: Bodies of Evidence: Autopsies and the Rise of Medical Examiners

1. Stratmoen, *Murder, Mayhem, and Mystery*, 51.

2. Ibid.

3. Ibid., 168.

4. David Leafe, "Solved: How the Brides in the Bath Died at the Hands of Their Ruthless Womanising Husband," *Daily Mail* (London), April 22, 2010, http://www.dailymail.co.uk/femail/article-1267913/Solved-How-brides-bath-died-hands-ruthless-womaniser.html.

5. Kate Colquhoun, review of *The Magnificent Spilsbury and the Case of the Brides in the Bath*, by Jane Robins, *Telegraph* (London), June 7, 2010, http://www.telegraph.co.uk/culture/books/bookreviews/7801091/The-Magnificent-Spilsbury-and-the-Case-of-the-Brides-in-the-Bath-by-Jane-Robins-review.html.

6. Burney and Pemberton, "Bruised Witness," under "Spillsbury's Spell and Thorne's Martyrdom."

7. Ibid., under "Introduction."

8. Ibid.

9. Marten, *The Doctor Looks at Murder*, 274.

10. "Six Deaths Result from Arsenic Pie," *New York Times*, August 2, 1922, http://query.nytimes.com/mem/archive-free/pdf?res=940 DEFD71239EF3ABC4A53DFBE668389639EDE.

11. Ibid.

12. Marten, *The Doctor Looks at Murder*, 176.

13. Ibid., 177.

14. Ibid.

15. Ibid.

Chapter 3: Elementary, My Dear Watson: The First Detectives

1. Vidocq, *Memoirs of Vidocq*, 31.

2. "Scotland Yard to Use Women Sleuths," *Lewiston* (ME) *Daily Sun*, (AP), August 18, 1933, http://news.google.com/newspapers?nid=1928&dat=19330818&id=CM0gAAAAIBAJ&sjid=2WoFA AAAIBAJ&pg=3932,3334279.

3. Doyle, *A Study in Scarlet*, 6.

4. Ibid., 10.

5. Ibid., 20.

6. Ibid., 25.

7. Liebow, *Dr. Joe Bell*, 4.

Chapter 4: Not without a Trace: The Introduction of Crime Scene Evidence

1. Gross, *Criminal Investigation*, 2–3.

2. Dunphy and Cummins, *Remarkable Trials of All Countries*, 404.

3. Bell, *Encyclopedia of Forensic Science*, 234.

4. Thorwald, *Crime and Science*, 254.

5. Ibid., 255.

6. Ibid., 268.

7. David J. Krajicek, "Snagged by a Cord in Killing of Novelist," *New York Daily News*, October 31, 2009, http://www.nydailynews. com/news/crime/snagged-cord-killing-novelist-article-1.418391.

Chapter 5: Fingerprints Are Forever: Early Fingerprint Evidence

1. Henry Faulds, "On the Skin-Furrows of the Hand." Nature 22, 605-605 (28 October 1880) | www.nature.com/nature/journal/ v22/n574/abs/022605a0.html

2. H. O. Thompson, "Schwartz, Slayer, Suicide, Led Double Life; To Women He Was Harold Warren, War Hero," *Independent* (St. Petersburg, FL), August 11, 1925, https://news.google.com/ newspapers?nid=950&dat=19250811&id=fOFPAAAAIBAJ& sjid= hIQDAAAAIBAJ&pg=1594,6864764&hl=en.

3. Associated Press, "Man Who Faked Death Caught; Ends His Life," *Southeast Missourian*, August 10, 1925, https://news.google.com/ newspapers?nid=1893&dat=19250810&id=KXdFAAAAIBAJ&sjid =N8cMAAAAIBAJ&pg=4904,952091&hl=en.

4. Nickell and Fischer, *Crime Science*, 136.

Chapter 6: Bang! Bang! You're Dead: The Birth of Firearm Analysis

1. Jim Fisher, "The Stielow Firearms Identification Case," January 7, 2008, http://jimfisher.edinboro.edu/forensics/stielow.html.

2. Nickell and Fischer, *Crime Science*, 103.

3. Frankfurter, "The Case of Sacco and Vanzetti."

4. Ibid.

5. Ibid.

6. Ibid.

7. Ibid.

8. Doug Linder, "Sacco-Vanzetti."

9. Ibid.

10. Jim Fisher, "The St. Valentine's Day Massacre in the History of Forensic Ballistics," *Jim Fisher True Crime* (blog), February 14, 2015, http://jimfishertruecrime.blogspot.com/2013/07/the-st-valentines-day-massacre-in.html.

11. Marten, *The Doctor Looks at Murder*, 198.

12. "Crowley Indicted Quickly for Murder; Girl Aids the State," *New York Times*, May 9, 1931.

13. "Police Slayer Captured in Gun and Tear Gas Siege; 10,000 Watch in W. 90th St.," *New York Times*, May 8, 1931.

14. Ibid.

15. "Crowley Dies Blaming Girl for Execution," *Brooklyn Daily Eagle*, January 2, 1932, http://bklyn.newspapers.com/newspage/57286602/.

16. Kate Wells, "New Chapter in Bizarre Detroit Murder Case," *Here & Now* (WBUR Boston), radio transcript, August 13, 2013, http://hereandnow.wbur.org/2013/08/13/detroit-murder-case.

17. Marten, *The Doctor Looks at Murder*, 266.

18. Ibid., 267.

Chapter 7: Blood Is Thicker: The First Blood Pattern Cases

1. Thorwald, *Crime and Science*, 130.

2. Ibid., 130–131.

3. Ibid., 131.

4. Linder, "Dr. Sam Sheppard Trials."

5. Ibid.

6. "Why Isn't Sam Sheppard in Jail?" *The Cleveland Press.*

7. State v. Sheppard, 6269–70.

8. Ibid., 6272–73.

9. Linder, "Dr. Sam Sheppard Trials."

10. Ibid.

11. McCrary and Ramsland, *The Unknown Darkness,* 275.

12. Ragle, *Crime Scene,* 211.

13. Associated Press, "Ex-Dancer Booked in Mansion Slaying," *Tuscaloosa* (AL) *News,* January 6, 1964, https://news.google.com/ newspapers?nid=1817&dat=19640106&id=nSUeAAAAIBAJ& sjid=_ZoEAAAAIBAJ&pg=6155,613664&hl=en

14. Thorwald, *Crime and Science,* 226.

15. Ibid., 228.

16. Ibid., 229.

Chapter 8: Grave Matters: Hidden Bodies

1. Zugibe and Carroll, *Dissecting Death,* 19.

Chapter 10: To Catch a Killer: Criminal Profilers

1. Evans and Skinner, *Ultimate Jack the Ripper Companion,* 98.

2. Ibid., 184.

3. Ibid., 192.

4. Ibid., 187–188.

5. Ibid., 360.

6. Ibid., 361.

7. Ibid., 361–362.

8. "The Silence of the Lambs," *The Real Story*, Smithsonian Channel, May 2, 2010.

9. Ibid.

10. McCrary and Ramsland, *Unknown Darkness*, 137.

11. William Hermann, "Temple Massacre Has Had Lasting Impact." *Arizona Republic*, August 14, 2011, http://archive. azcentral.com/arizonarepublic/local/articles/20110814buddhist-temple-murders-west-valley-impact.html.

Chapter 11: One in a Trillion: The Dawn of DNA Evidence

1. Chris Harvey, in discussion with the author, November 2014.

2. Ibid.

3. Hilary Hurd Anyaso, "Savory Files Court Documents as Proof of Innocence," *Northwestern University News*, January 22, 2015, www.northwestern.edu/newscenter/stories/2015/01/savory-files-court-documents-as-proof-of-innocence.html.

4. People of the State of New York v. Roy A. Brown, 4.

5. Ibid.

6. "National Academy of Sciences Urges Comprehensive Reform of U.S. Forensic Sciences," Innocence Project, January 18, 2009, www.innocenceproject.org/news-events-exonerations/press-releases/national-academy-of-sciences-urges-comprehensive-reform-of-u-s-forensic-sciences.

7. People of the State of New York v. Roy A. Brown, 7.

Bibliography

Primary Sources

Adams, Charles F. *Murder by the Bay: Historic Homicide in and about the City of San Francisco.* Sanger, CA: Quill Driver Books, 2005.

Associated Press. "Man Who Faked Death Caught; Ends His Life." *Southeast Missourian,* August 10, 1925. www.news.google.com/newspapers?nid=1893&dat=19250810&id=KXdFAAAAIBAJ &sjid= N8cMAAAAIBAJ&pg=4904,9520091&hl=en.

Bostrom, Karl. "Dr. Gettler Takes Tiny Clues and Solves Big Murder Cases." *New York Post,* April 25, 1936. www.fultonhistory .com/newspaper%2011/New%20York%20Evening%20Post/ New%20York%20NY%20Evening%20Post%201936%20 Grayscale/New%20York%20NY%20Evening%20Post%20 1936%20Grayscale%20-%202724.pdf.

Brooklyn Daily Eagle. "Crowley Dies Blaming Girl for Execution." January

2, 1932. www.bklyn.newspapers.com/newspage/57286602.

Chicago Daily Tribune. "Suicide Reveals Killing and Hoax to Grab $100,000." August 10, 1925. http://archives.chicagotribune.com/1925/08/10/page/3/article/suicide-reveals-killing-and-hoax-to-grab-100-000.

Douglas, John, and Mark Olshaker. *Mind Hunter.* New York: Simon & Schuster, 1995.

Doyle, Sir Arthur Conan. *A Study in Scarlet.* San Diego: Canterbury Classics, 2011.

Dunphy, Thomas, and Thomas J. Cummins. *Remarkable Trials of All Countries: Particularly of the United States, Great Britain, Ireland and France; with Notes and Speeches of Counsel Containing Thrilling Narratives of Fact from the Court Room, also Historical Reminiscences of Wonderful Events.* New York: Diossy & Company, 1870.

Eckert, William. "Medicolegal Investigation in New York City." *The American Journal of Forensic Medicine and Pathology* 4:1 (March 1983). http://journals.lww.com/amjforensicmedicine/Abstract/1983/03000/Medicolegal_investigation_in_New_York_City_.5.aspx.

Erzinçlioğlu, Dr. Zakaria. *Maggots, Murder, and Men: Memories and Reflections of a Forensic Entomologist.* New York: St. Martin's, 2000.

Evans, Stewart P., and Keith Skinner. *The Ultimate Jack the Ripper Companion.* New York: Carroll & Graf, 2000.

Frankfurter, Felix. "The Case of Sacco and Vanzetti." *The Atlantic,* March 1927. www.theatlantic.com/magazine/archive/1927/03/the-case-of-sacco-and-vanzetti/306625/?single_page=true.

Glassie, Henry Haywood, and Wilfred M. Barton. "A Notice of the New Method of Distinguishing Human from Other Blood

Stains." *Washington Law Reporter* 29 (1901): 384–85. www.books
.google.com/books?id=Q9QZAAAAYAAJ&pg=PA385&dq=
human+blood+test+rabbit+serum&hl=en&sa=X&ei=GJtcVb
jcFsKZyATBmYDwDQ&ved=0CDUQ6AEwAQ#v=onepage
&q=human%20blood%20test%20rabbit%20serum&f=false.

Gross, Hans. *Criminal Investigation: A Practical Handbook for Magistrates,
Police Officers, and Lawyers.* Translated and adapted to Indian Colonial Practice by John Adam and John Collyer Adam. Egmore,
India: A. Krishnamachari, 1906. https://archive.org/details/
criminalinvestig00grosuoft.

Hutchinson (KS) *News.* "Admits Plot to Collect Big Insurance Policy."
August 10, 1925. www.newspapers.com/image/8461987/?terms
=charles%2Bschwartz%2Bwarren%2Bbarbe%2Bbody%
2Bidentified.

Lewiston (ME) *Daily Sun.* "Scotland Yard to Use Women Sleuths." August
18, 1933. www.news.google.com/newspapers?nid=1928&dat=
19330818&id=CM0gAAAAIBAJ&sjid=2WoFAAAAIBAJ
&pg=3932,3334279.

Lydon, Christopher. "J. Edgar Hoover Made the F.B.I. Formidable
with Politics, Publicity and Results." Obituary. *New York Times,*
May 3, 1972. www.nytimes.com/learning/general/onthisday/
bday/0101.html.

Marten, M. Edward, as told to Norman Cross. *The Doctor Looks at
Murder.* New York: Doubleday, Doran & Company, 1937.

McCrary, Gregg O., with Katherine Ramsland. *The Unknown Darkness: Profiling the Predators among Us.* New York: William Morrow,
2003.

New York Times. "7 Chicago Gangsters Slain by Firing Squad of Rivals,

Some in Police Uniforms." February 14, 1929. www.nytimes .com/learning/general/onthisday/big/0214.html.

———. "Accuses Dr. W. T. Scheele." June 6, 1896. http://query .nytimes.com/mem/archive-free/pdf?res=9E07E3DD1031E53 3A65755C0A9609C94679ED7CF.

———. "Crowley Indicted Quickly for Murder; Girl Aids the State." May 9, 1931.

———. "Dr. Hyde Arrested as Swope's Slayer." February 11, 1910. http://query.nytimes.com/mem/archive-free/pdf?res=9B01E0 DA1539E433A25752C1A9649C946196D6CF.

———. "Her Trial Nearly Over." June 19, 1896. http://query .nytimes.com/mem/archive-free/pdf?res=9D02E6D81338E23 3A2575AC1A9609C94679ED7CF.

———. "Mud on Bed a Clue in Titterton Case." April 14, 1936. http://query.nytimes.com/mem/archive/pdf?res=9D05EFD81 430E13BBC4C52DFB266838D629EDE.

———. "Police Slayer Captured in Gun and Tear Gas Siege; 10,000 Watch in W. 90th St." May 8, 1931.

———. "Sheds Tears in Court." June 3, 1896. http://query.nytimes .com/mem/archive-free/pdf?res=9E03E5D81338E533A65750 C0A9609C94679ED7CF.

———. "Six Deaths Result from Arsenic Pie." August 2, 1922. http://query.nytimes.com/mem/archive-free/pdf?res=940DEF D71239EF3ABC4A53DFBE668389639EDE.

———. "Sure Poisoned Pie Was Meant to Kill." August 3, 1922. http://query.nytimes.com/mem/archive-free/pdf?res=9C0DE FD61239EF3ABC4B53DFBE668389639EDE.

———. "Swope Poison Case Must Be Retried." April 12, 1911.

http://query.nytimes.com/mem/archivefree/pdf?res=9403EF
DEI03IE233A2575ICIA9629C946096D6CF.

————. "W. T. Scheele Attacked." June 17, 1896. http://query
.nytimes.com/mem/archive-free/pdf?res=9E0IE7DBIF38E53
3A65754CIA9609C94679ED7CF.

Oakland (CA) Tribune. "Schwartz, Trapped in Apartment, Shoots Self."
August 10, 1925. www.newspapers.com/image/90334072.

————. "Schwartz's Gay Life While Hiding Bared; Dates Set for
Inquest of Slayer, Victim." August 10, 1925. www.newspapers
.com/image/90334068.

Old Bailey Proceedings Online (www.oldbaileyonline.org, version 7.2,
23 November 2015), May 1905, trial of Alfred Stratton (22) Albert
Ernest Stratton (20) (t19050502-415). www.oldbaileyonline.org/
browse.jsp?id=t19050502-415&div=t19050502-415.

————, October 1910, trial of CRIPPEN, Hawley Harvey (48,
dentist) (t19101011-74). www.oldbaileyonline.org/browse.jsp?
id=t19101011-74-offence-1&div=t19101011-74#highlight.

Oregonian (Portland, OR). "More Swopes Died by Being Poisoned."
February 13, 1910. http://oregonnews.uoregon.edu/lccn/
sn83045782/1910-02-13/ed-1/seq-6.

People of the State of Illinois, Appellee, v. Johnny Lee Savory. No.:
88786. Supreme Court of Illinois. Decision. May 24, 2001.
http://caselaw.findlaw.com/il-supreme-court/1259598.html.

People of the State of New York v. Roy A. Brown. Indictment
No.: 91-46. State of New York, County of Cayuga. Affirma-
tion in Support of Motion to Vacate Conviction and Sentence
Pursuant to C.P.L. 444.10 (1-g) Linked by the New York
Times. December 21, 2006. www.nytimes.com/packages/pdf/

nyregion/2006122IBROWN_MOTION.doc.

Ragle, Larry. *Crime Scene: From Fingerprints to DNA Testing—an Astonishing Inside Look at the Real World of C.S.I.* New York: HarperCollins, 1995.

Sacco-Vanzetti Case: Transcript of the Record of the Trial of Nicola Sacco and Bartolomeo Vanzetti in the Courts of Massachusetts and Subsequent Proceedings, 1920–7, The. Vol. 5. Mamaroneck, NY: P. P. Appel, 1969.

Sale of Arsenic Regulation Act, 1851, 15 Vic (Eng). www.legislation .gov.uk/ukpga/1851/13/enacted.

State v. Hyde. 234 Mo. 200; 136 S.W. 316. Missouri Supreme Court. April 11, 1911. Reprinted in *The American and English Annotated Cases.* New York: Ward Thompson Company and San Francisco: Bancroft-Whitney Company, 1912. www.books.google.com/books ?id=5vlCAQAAMAAJ&pg=PA195&lpg=PA195&dq=hyde +swope+autopsies+traces+of+cyanide&source=bl&ots=kb sD4yINiz&sig=sqN5IuNcFs6DnnwNWCkHdItcuAE&hl= en&sa=X&ei=OPSuVK2ULoaSyQTCwYLICg&ved=0CCw Q6AEwAg#v=onepage&q=hyde%20swope%20autopsies%20 traces%20of%20cyanide&f=false.

State v. Sheppard. Testimony of Dr. Sam Sheppard. 1954. http:// engagedscholarship.csuohio.edu/sheppard_transcripts_1954/12.

Stratmoen, Mark R. *Murder, Mayhem, and Mystery: Coroner Inquests in Fremont County, Wyoming, 1885–1900.* Riverton, WY: Lenore Wyoming Publications, 2010.

Thompson, H. O. "Schwartz, Slayer, Suicide, Led Double Life; To Women He Was Harold Warren, War Hero." *Independent* (St. Petersburg, FL), August 11, 1925. www.news.google.com/ newspapers?nid=950&dat=19250811&id= fOFPAAAAIBAJ&

sjid=hIQDAAAAIBAJ&pg=1594,6864764&hl=en.

Thorwald, Jürgen. *Crime and Science: The New Frontier in Criminology.* Richard and Clara Winston, trans. New York: Harcourt, 1967.

Tuscaloosa (AL) *News.* "Ex-Dancer Booked in Mansion Slaying." January 6, 1964. www.news.google.com/newspapers?nid=1817&dat=19640106&id=nSUeAAAAIBAJ&sjid=_ZoEAAAAIBAJ&pg=6155,613664&hl=en.

Ubelaker, Douglas, and Henry Scammell. *Bones: A Forensic Detective's Casebook.* New York: M. Evans and Company, 1992.

US Department of Justice. "A Review of the FBI's Handling of the Brandon Mayfield Case." January 2006. www.justice.gov/oig/special/s0601/exec.pdf.

Vidocq, Eugène François. *Memoirs of Vidocq: Principal Agent of the French Police until 1827.* Translated from French. Philadelphia: E.L. Carey & A. Hart, 1834. www.books.google.com/books?id=uGQoAAAAYAAJ&printsec=titlepage#v=onepage&q=deloro&f=false.

"Why Isn't Sam Sheppard in Jail?" Editorial. *The Cleveland Press.* July 30, 1954. http://engagedscholarship.csuohio.edu/cgi/viewcontent.cgi?article=1005&context=sheppard_maxwell_articles.

Zugibe, Frederick, and David L. Carroll. *Dissecting Death: Secrets of a Medical Examiner.* New York: Broadway Books, 2005.

Secondary Sources

Anyaso, Hilary Hurd. "Savory Files Court Documents as Proof of Innocence." *Northwestern University News,* January 22, 2015. www.northwestern.edu/newscenter/stories/2015/01/savory-files-court-documents-as-proof-of-innocence.html.

Bahn, Paul G. *Written in Bones: How Human Remains Unlock the Secrets of the Dead.* Toronto, Ontario: Firefly, 2003.

Bailey, Brianna. "A Look Back: Millionaire Died in Misunderstanding." *Daily Pilot* (Fountain Valley, CA), October 10, 2009. http://articles.dailypilot.com/2009-10-10/features/dpt-alookback101109_1_millionaires-newport-beach-mansion.

Balko, Radley. "It Literally Started with a Witch Hunt: A History of Bite Mark Evidence." *The Washington Post*, February 17, 2015. www.washingtonpost.com/news/the-watch/wp/2015/02/17/it-literally-started-with-a-witch-hunt-a-history-of-bite-mark-evidence.

Barnes, Jeffery. "History." In *The Fingerprint Sourcebook.* Washington, DC: US Department of Justice Office of Justice Programs, 2014. www.ncjrs.gov/pdffiles1/nij/225321.pdf.

Bell, Suzanne. *Encyclopedia of Forensic Science.* New York: Facts on File, 2008.

Biography. "Hawley Crippen." www.biography.com/people/hawley-crippen-17172114.

Blumber, Jess. "A Brief History of Scotland Yard." Smithsonian Online. September 27, 2007. www.smithsonianmag.com/history/a-brief-history-of-scotland-yard-172669755/?no-ist.

Brady Campaign. "About Gun Violence." www.bradycampaign.org/about-gun-violence.

British Transport Police. "The first railway murder." www.btp.police.uk/about_us/our_history/crime_history/the_first_railway_murder.aspx.

Burney, Ian. "Our Environment in Miniature: Dust and the Early Twentieth-Century Forensic Imagination." *Representations* (Winter

2013). www.ncbi.nlm.nih.gov/pmc/articles/PMC3678505.

Burney, Ian, and Neil Pemberton. "Bruised Witness: Bernard Spilsbury and the Performance of Early Twentieth-Century English
Forensic Pathology." *Medical History* (January 2011). www.ncbi
.nlm.nih.gov/pmc/articles/PMC3037214.

Cale, Cynthia. "Forensic DNA Evidence Is Not Infallible." *Nature*,
November 5, 2015. www.nature.com/news/forensic-dna-evidence-
is-not-infallible-1.18654.

Cavendish, Richard. "Tsar Nicholas II and His Family Were Murdered on July 17th, 1918." *History Today* 58:7 (July 7, 2008). www
.historytoday.com/richard-cavendish/murders-ekaterinburg.

Cicetti, Fred. "What's the Most Common Blood Type?" Live Science.
July 13, 2012. www.livescience.com/36559-common-blood-type-
donation.html.

Colquhoun, Kate. Review of *The Magnificent Spilsbury and the Case of the
Brides in the Bath* by Jane Robins. *Telegraph* (London), June 7, 2010.
www.telegraph.co.uk/culture/books/bookreviews/7801091/
The-Magnificent-Spilsbury-and-the-Case-of-the-Brides-in-the-
Bath-by-Jane-Robins-review.html.

Crime Museum. "John Dillinger-Fingerprint Obliteration." www
.crimemuseum.org/blog/john-dillinger-fingerprint-obliteration.

DiBiase, Thomas. "'No-body' Murder Trials in the United States."
No Body Murder Cases. November 20, 2014. www.nobodycases
.com/cases.html.

Duramy, Benedetta Faedi. "Women and Poisons in 17th Century
France." *Chicago-Kent Law Review* 87:2 (April 2012): 347–70.
http://scholarship.kentlaw.iit.edu/cgi/viewcontent.cgi?article=
3837&context=cklawreview.

Edwards, Samuel. *The Vidocq Dossier: The Story of the World's First Detective.* Boston: Houghton Mifflin, 1977.

Emsley, John. *Elements of Murder: A History of Poison.* Oxford: Oxford University Press, 2005.

FBI. "Next Generation Identification." www.fbi.gov/about-us/cjis/ fingerprints_biometrics/ngi.

Felch, Jason. "Solving Crimes Using Fingerprints Is an Inexact Science." *Los Angeles Times*, March 20, 2009. http://articles.latimes. com/2009/mar/20/opinion/oe-felch20.

Fisher, Jim. "Fingerprints." Jim Fisher. http://jimfisher.edinboro .edu/forensics/fire/print.html.

———. "Firearms Identification in the Sacco-Vanzetti Case Part II." Jim Fisher. http://jimfisher.edinboro.edu/forensics/ sacco2_2.html

———. "The St. Valentine's Day Massacre in the History of Forensic Ballistics." *Jim Fisher True Crime* (blog), February 14, 2015. http://jimfishertruecrime.blogspot.com/2013/07/the-st-valentines-day-massacre-in.html.

———. "The Stielow Firearms Identification Case." Jim Fisher. January 7, 2008. http://jimfisher.edinboro.edu/forensics/stielow .html.

Fowler, Giles. *Deaths on Pleasant Street: The Ghastly Enigma of Colonel Swope and Doctor Hyde.* Kirksville, MO: Truman State University Press, 2009.

Glionna, John. "Man convicted in 1991 Phoenix-Area Buddhist Temple Massacre." *Los Angeles Times*, January 23, 2014. http:// articles.latimes.com/2014/jan/23/nation/la-na-buddhist-temple-conviction-20140124.

Goff, M. Lee. *A Fly for the Prosecution: How Insect Evidence Helps Solve Crimes.* Cambridge, MA: Harvard University Press, 2000.

Hagen, Carrie. "The Big Mystery behind the Great Train Robbery May Finally Have Been Solved." Smithsonian Online. July 16, 2014. www.smithsonianmag.com/history/big-mystery-behind-great-train-robbery-may-finally-been-solved-180952054/?no-ist.

Hall, Stephen S. "Last Hours of the Iceman." *National Geographic,* July 2007. http://ngm.nationalgeographic.com/2007/07/iceman/hall-text/1.

Heinzelman, Susan Sage, and Zipporah Batshaw Wiseman, eds. *Representing Women: Law, Literature, and Feminism.* Durham, NC: Duke University Press, 1994.

Hermann, William. "Temple Massacre Has Had Lasting Impact." *The Arizona Republic,* August 14, 2011. http://archive.azcentral.com/arizonarepublic/local/articles/20110814buddhist-temple-murders-west-valley-impact.html.

Heslop, Paul. *Murderous Women: From Sarah Dazley to Ruth Ellis.* Stroud, UK: The History Press, 2009.

History. "Fingerprint Evidence Is Used to Solve a British Murder Case." This Day in History. 2009. www.history.com/this-day-in-history/fingerprint-evidence-is-used-to-solve-a-british-murder-case.

Hsu, Jeremy. "Case Closed on Murders of Last Russian Czar's Family." Live Science. March 2, 2009. www.livescience.com/7693-case-closed-murders-russian-czars-family.html.

Hsu, Spencer. "FBI Admits Flaws in Hair Analysis Over Decades." *The Washington Post,* April 18, 2015. www.washingtonpost.com/local/crime/fbi-overstated-forensic-hair-matches-in-nearly-

all-criminal-trials-for-decades/2015/04/18/39c8d8c6-e515-
11e4-b510-962fcfabc310_story.html.

Hughes, Caroline. "Challenges in DNA Testing and Forensic Analysis of Hair Samples." *Forensic Magazine,* April 2, 2013. www
.forensicmag.com/articles/2013/04/challenges-dna-testing-
and-forensic-analysis-hair-samples.

Innocence Project. "Access to Post-Conviction DNA Testing."
October 10, 2014. www.innocenceproject.org/free-innocent/
improve-the-law/fact-sheets/access-to-post-conviction-dna-
testing.

———. "FBI Testimony on Microscopic Hair Analysis Contained
Errors in at Least 90 Percent of Cases in Ongoing Review," April
20, 2015. www.innocenceproject.org/news-events-exonerations/
press-releases/fbi-testimony-on-microscopic-hair-analysis-
contained-errors-in-at-least-90-of-cases-in-ongoing-review.

———. "National Academy of Sciences Urges Comprehensive
Reform of US Forensic Sciences." January 18, 2009. www
.innocenceproject.org/news-events-exonerations/press-releases/
national-academy-of-sciences-urges-comprehensive-reform-of-u-
s-forensic-sciences.

———. "The Causes of Wrongful Conviction." www.innocence-
project.org/causes-wrongful-conviction.

International Hunter Education Association. "Caliber and Gauge."
http://homestudy.ihea.com/aboutfirearms/22a_calibergauge
.htm.

Krajicek, David J. "Snagged by a Cord in Killing of Novelist." *New
York Daily News.* October 31, 2009. www.nydailynews.com/news/
crime/snagged-cord-killing-novelist-article-1.418391.

Kurland, Michael. *Irrefutable Evidence: Adventures in the History of Forensic Science.* Chicago: Ivan R. Dee, 2009.

Lange, Karen E. "Tales from the Bog." *National Geographic,* September 2007. http://ngm.nationalgeographic.com/2007/09/bog-bodies/bog-bodies-text/I.

Leafe, David. "Solved: How the Brides in the Bath Died at the Hands of their Ruthless Womanising Husband." *Daily Mail* (London), April 22, 2010. www.dailymail.co.uk/femail/article-1267913/Solved-How-brides-bath-died-hands-ruthless-womaniser.html.

Liebow, Ely. *Dr. Joe Bell: Model for Sherlock Holmes* Madison, WI: University of Wisconsin Press, 2007.

Linder, Doug. "Dr. Sam Sheppard Trials." Famous Trials. 2006. http://law2.umkc.edu/faculty/projects/ftrials/sheppard/samsheppardtrial.html.

———. "The Sacco-Vanzetti Case: An Account." Famous Trials. 2001. http://law2.umkc.edu/faculty/projects/ftrials/SaccoV/SaccoV.htm.

Livingston, James D. *Arsenic and Clam Chowder: Murder in Gilded Age New York.* Albany: State University of New York Press, 2010.

Lorenzi, Rossella. "The Iceman Suffered Brain Damage Before Death." *Discovery News* (blog), June 10, 2013. www.news.discovery.com/history/the-iceman-suffered-brain-damage-before-death-130610.htm.

Lubet, Steven. *Murder in Tombstone: The Forgotten Trial of Wyatt Earp.* New Haven, CT: Yale University Press, 2004.

Mariner, Brian. *On Death's Bloody Trail: Murder and the Art of Forensic Science.* New York: St. Martin's Press, 1993.

McBride, Alex. "Miranda v. Arizona." *Supreme Court History.* PBS.

www.pbs.org/wnet/supremecourt/rights/landmark_miranda .html.

Mears, Bill. "Supreme Court: DNA Swab after Arrest Is Legitimate Search." CNN, June 4, 2013. www.cnn.com/2013/06/03/ justice/supreme-court-dna-tests.

National Registry of Exonerations. "Roy Brown." University Michigan Law School. June 2012. www.law.umich.edu/special/ exoneration/Pages/casedetail.aspx?caseid=3064.

Nickell, Joe, and John F. Fischer. *Crime Science: Methods of Forensic Detection.* Lexington, KY: The University Press of Kentucky, 1999.

O'Brien, John. "The St. Valentine's Day Massacre." *Chicago Tribune,* February 14, 2014. http://articles.chicagotribune.com/ 2014-02-14/news/chi-chicagodays-valentinesmassacre-story_1_al-capone-smc-cartage-co-george-bugs-moran.

Oien, Cary. "Forensic Hair Comparison: Background Information for Interpretation." *Forensic Science Communications* 11:2 (April 2009). www.fbi.gov/about-us/lab/forensic-science-communications/ fsc/april2009/review/2009_04_review02.htm.

Old Bailey Online. "Policing in London." www.oldbaileyonline.org/ static/Policing.jsp.

Owen, James. "5 Surprising Facts about Otzi the Iceman." *National Geographic,* October 18, 2013. http://news.nationalgeographic. com/news/2013/10/131016-otzi-ice-man-mummy-five-facts.

Pinkerton. "History." www.pinkerton.com/history.

Ramsland, Katherine. *The Devil's Dozen: 12 Notorious Serial Killers Caught by Cutting-Edge Forensics.* New York: Berkley Books, 2009.

Real Story, The. "The Silence of the Lambs." Smithsonian Channel, aired May 2, 2010.

Red Cross, The. "Blood Types." www.redcrossblood.org/learn-about-blood/blood-types.

Ross, Valerie. "Forget Fingerprints: Law Enforcement DNA Databases Poised to Expand." *Nova,* PBS. January 2, 2014. www.pbs.org/wgbh/nova/next/body/dna-databases.

Ryder, Stephen P., ed. "Mary Ann Nichols." Casebook: Jack the Ripper. www.casebook.org/victims/polly.html.

Saks, Michael J. "Forensic Identification: From a Faith-Based 'Science' to a Scientific Science." *Forensic Science International,* April 2010. www.fsijournal.org/article/S0379-0738(10)00106-4/fulltext.

Schiff, Neal. "Murder Conviction; No Body Found." *Inside the FBI,* podcast transcript. September 18, 2009. www.fbi.gov/news/podcasts/inside/murder-conviction-no-body-found.mp3/view.

Schmidt, John. "Death Comes for the Archbishop." WBEZ. *Chicago History Today* (blog), February 10, 2012. www.wbez.org/blog/john-r-schmidt/2012-02-10/death-comes-archbishop-96087.

Sohn, Emily. "Ice Mummy May Have Smashed Eye in Fall." *Discovery News,* November 21, 2011. www.news.discovery.com/history/archaeology/iceman-oetzi-eye-injury-111121.htm.

South Tyrol Museum of Archaeology. "Ötzi—the Iceman." 2013. www.iceman.it/en/when-oetzi-died.

Spitz, Werner. *Spitz & Fischer's Medicolegal Investigation of Death: Guidelines for the Application of Pathology to Crime Investigation,* 3rd ed. Springfield, IL: Charles C. Thomas, 1993.

Starr, Douglas. "CSI 1881: The Birth of Forensics." *Discover Magazine,* February 28, 2011. www.discovermagazine.com/2010/nov/22-csi-original-the-birth-of-forensics.

Svoboda, Elizabeth. "The Early Days of Toxicology: Poisonous Powder." *New York Times*, May 11, 2009. www.nytimes.com/2009/05/12/science/12file-arsenic.html?_r=0.

University of Tennessee Knoxville. "The Forensic Anthropology Center." http://web.utk.edu/~fac.

Vergano, Dan. "DNA Upends Century-Old Murder Verdict." *USA Today*, January 1, 2011. http://usatoday30.usatoday.com/tech/science/columnist/vergano/2011-01-09-crippen-dna_N.htm.

Wade, Stephen. *Plain Clothes and Sleuths: A History of Detectives in Britain.* Stroud, UK: The History Press, 2007.

Ward, Susannah. *Secrets of Scotland Yard.* Arlington, VA: PBS, 2013. DVD.

Wells, Kate. "New Chapter in Bizarre Detroit Murder Case." *Here & Now*, WBUR Boston, radio transcript. August 13, 2013. www.hereandnow.wbur.org/2013/08/13/detroit-murder-case.

Whitechapel Society, The. *Jack the Ripper: The Suspects.* Stroud, UK: The History Press, 2012.

Photo Credits

Acknowledgments

During school visits, younger students often ask how I made the book, as in the actual physical copy. I tell them somebody else does that, and that writing is only one part of the work that goes into making a book. With that in mind, I'd like to thank:

Kelly Sonnack for representing me in this project and telling me about it in the first place.

Donna Bray for coming up with the great idea for this book and ushering it through all the stages of revising and editing.

Viana Siniscalchi for procuring photos and helping every step of the way.

HarperCollins copy editors, proofreaders, designers, marketers, salespeople, and more for turning the manuscript into a book and getting that book into the hands of readers.

Chris Harvey for walking me through the process of investigating cold cases using DNA evidence.

Kay Sirianni for shedding light on the forensic science described in several areas of the book.

My parents for instilling in me a love of stories.

My husband, Justin, for supporting me through all the crazy ups and downs of being a writer!

Index

Page numbers in *italics* refer to illustrations.